Karate:
The Energy Connection

Karate:
The Energy Connection

by W. Scott Russell

Delacorte Press | Eleanor Friede

Manufactured in the United States of America
Second Printing—1977

Library of Congress Cataloging in Publication Data

Russell, W. Scott , 1946–
    Karate: the energy connection.

    Bibliography: p.
    Íncludes index.
    1. Karate. I. Title.
GV1114.3.R87   796.8'153   76–5824
ISBN 0–440–04386–7

*To the further study of the individual,
the primitive as well as the intellectual . . .
and to the thousands of teachers who believe in their art,
continue to learn, and give up their time and energies
for the future of karate.*

Contents

10. *Karate for the Western World*   *178*

11. *Choosing a Karate School*   *194*

Acknowledgments

The making of a book is a great learning experience, an organizer of thought. I hope this book will be as valuable to its readers as it has been to me.

I would like to express my gratitude to all those who have helped in the creation of this book. Particularly to Eleanor Friede, who directed its course. To Martin Edelston, who gave up time from his busy schedule. To Gary Benner, who was the sounding board for many of the theories presented in the book. To Allen Good, for his understanding and enthusiasm. To Jimmy and Millie Cavanaugh, who were always willing to help in any way. To my brother Jack, for his continued interest in and support of my projects.

And especially to Harvey Ardman, who gave ideas a center, gave concepts and information a structure, for the patience and warmth he displayed in the many hours we worked together, for putting it all together into readable form.

Chapter 1

A Journey Toward Self-Fulfillment

The book you're about to read is a result of my strongly held conviction that every American—man, woman, and child—can benefit from learning karate, whether or not they're seeking a method of self-defense.

I hope to convince you that you can improve your life in many different ways, some of them extraordinarily significant and profound, if you take up karate and make it a part of your life. With this purpose in mind, I intend to show you

- Just what karate is and what it isn't (there are a lot of misconceptions floating around, some of them pretty ridiculous—though very widely held)
- What philosophical principles underlie the art and

how—though they're ancient and Oriental—they're
totally relevant for America today
- What karate can do for you physically, both in terms
  of physical fitness and better health
- What karate can do for you mentally, both in the
  intellectual and the emotional sense
- How karate can help you in your everyday life, in
  your relationships with people, at work and at home
- How you can use karate to protect yourself against
  violence
- How karate can improve your sex life

I also discuss just who can learn karate and how to
decide where to go for instruction. And in this process,
I give you a taste of karate itself—an appetizer that will
give you some idea what karate can feel like, both mentally and physically.

If you're seeking physical fitness, or the ability to
deal with stress, or a way to get out of your mental low,
or a path to greater vitality, or a method of achieving an
inner calm or peace, or a technique for using all your
abilities all the time, karate may be exactly what you're
looking for.

I think I should also tell you here what I *don't* intend
this book to do:

I don't intend it to give you the impression that
karate can solve all your problems—mental, physical,
emotional, social, etc.—though I believe that if you give
karate half a chance, it can do wonders for you.

I also don't intend it to make you into a black belt
karateist. My object here is not to teach karate, but to
describe it, to demonstrate its benefits and advantages.

A word of caution is in order at this point about how

I use the word "karate" throughout this book. I'm using the word to represent *all* the Oriental martial arts. I'm using it broadly and generically, as the American public usually does, even though karate is a word that refers to a specific martial art form. I'm doing this as a matter of convenience and communication.

My Story and Yours

In a sense, this book is two stories—my story and your story. It begins with me: how and why I became interested in karate, what it taught me, how it changed my life, how I saw it change others' lives. And it continues with your story: what karate can teach you, how it can change your life, how it can bring you so many of the things we all strive for: mental and physical fitness, self-confidence and self-awareness, even fulfillment and inner peace.

My story begins more than twenty years ago, during my formative years, in a suburban New Jersey town not far from New York City. It was there that I attended elementary school, that I grew up.

For most kids, I suppose, elementary school is a time when you learn the basics—reading, writing, and arithmetic, and how to get along with your peers. But there was one more subject in the curriculum my school offered: survival.

I grew up in a rough neighborhood, a lower-middle-class neighborhood. The tensions and frictions were out in the open here; there was no way to avoid them, even if you were only eight or nine years old. Looking back on it now, it seems to me that I not only went to school,

I went to war—and certainly not a war of my own choosing.

Every morning I left the house wondering if I could make it to class without having to defend myself. I felt like people in wagon trains must have felt on their way through the Sioux nation. The fear was really intense. And it wasn't just a matter of imagination, either.

I couldn't always avoid my tormentors. Fortunately, a young man who lived in the apartment above ours took me under his wing and appointed himself my big brother. I was badly in need of that kind of support, since my mother and father had separated and I was living with my mother, my two sisters, and my grandmother.

The young man who lived in our building—Danny—was a semiprofessional boxer. When he saw what was happening to me, he taught me the rudiments of boxing. By that time, I was a stocky, gutsy little boy, with a fair amount of street savvy. Boxing didn't make me into the terror of the school—not by a long shot—but it helped me give as good as I was getting.

It was about this time that the family moved, to a nearby town that couldn't have been more different from where I'd been living, an upper-middle-class area where schools were learning institutions, not combat zones. You might think that my life took a sudden turn for the better, that I was easily able to fit into the community and that I did well with my peers. Not so. I'd learned a skill—and an attitude—in my old home town that wasn't appropriate here. I was ready and able to fight to protect myself, but there no longer was any threat.

In short, I was trained for a different kind of world. I didn't know how to act in this new environment, where arguments were verbal but rarely physical, where people said please and thank you, where there was no reason to be afraid at ten minutes to three.

So I had my troubles. I didn't make the adjustment easily. I had problems at school, both socially and with the work. And I didn't know what to do with myself. I was still at loose ends by the time I graduated from high school. I didn't know what to do with my life. My aims and goals were unclear to me.

Remembering, perhaps, what boxing had done for me as a youngster, I found myself turning to similar activities. Finally I tried karate. That was ten years ago.

During the decade since, I have gone from a karate student who paid for his lessons by working as a janitor at the school, to an instructor, to the owner of two karate schools in northern New Jersey that, between them, have many hundreds of students. I have also progressed from white belt—beginner—through the various grades, learning different approaches and different skills from several teachers. I now hold black belt ratings in a number of systems.

But karate has given me more than just an occupation and a collection of certificates. It has given me a meaning and purpose in life—to a degree I never thought possible.

Karate has made me into the person I always wanted to be. It has given me a profound sense of self-awareness and self-confidence, leading me toward the full use of all my abilities, bringing me a deep feeling of self-fulfillment and inner peace. Moreover, as I've grown within myself, my relations with other people have improved. Those painful high school days are only a memory now. I'm at ease with myself and with my friends and colleagues.

If I'd merely taken karate as a self-improvement pro-

gram, as an evening activity to supplement a full-time
career or job in some other field, I might be tempted to
say that its effects on me were a result of my own particular personality or psychological makeup. But I've
been associated with karate instruction for many years
now, and I've been in a unique position to see its effects
on others—literally thousands of others.

Promises and Possibilities

Karate doesn't change everyone's life. Some people are
in fine shape—mentally and physically—when they start
it. Some don't give it a decent trial. But it has an enormous impact on almost everyone who's willing to give it
some time and energy.

Let me tell you what some of my students have said
about karate and how it has changed their lives:

> "Karate has made me see that I'm mentally
> stronger than I thought I was. I think it's made me
> a far more effective person on the job" (a trial
> lawyer).
> "Karate has given me a better understanding of
> people. And that's helped me in my relationships on
> the job and off" (a nurse's aide).
> "I think karate has increased my powers of con-
> centration and my clarity of thought" (a computer
> programmer).
> "Karate has made me feel years younger. It's
> given me a new vitality. It's even helped my sex life"
> (owner of an appliance store).
> "I've lost seventeen pounds since I took up karate.

And that was six months ago. It's the first time in my life I've been able to keep weight off" (salesman in a department store).

"Now that I know something about karate, I feel safer. I don't think of myself as a patsy anymore" (a housewife).

"I used to mope around the house all day, not feeling like doing anything. Now I've gotten myself involved in a half-dozen different things—football, a job on Saturdays—I'm even doing my homework these days. It seems to me karate is the cause of it all" (a high school senior).

"Before I started karate, I was a nervous fellow. Jumpy, you know, unsettled. Now I have—I don't know how to describe it—a kind of inner calm. It's like I'm in control of my life" (an assembly worker at an electronics plant).

I've heard statements like these from almost everyone who's attended one of my schools or who's had any real experience with karate. And I've seen people change, with my own eyes.

It's what I've seen happen to myself and others during the study of karate that has led me, in part, to write this book. I feel there's far more to karate than most people realize. I believe it could change many, if not most, lives for the better.

Who Can Learn Karate

Contrary to popular opinion, karate is not the "sport of killers." In fact, the impulsively violent person, the impatient mentality, is a poor karate student because he doesn't have the proper mental set for learning the art. He has the wrong ideas about fighting. His thinking is distorted. Although he may be intelligent, he is not wise.

People who resort to impulsive violence are too lazy to think. They're like little children who throw temper tantrums to get what they want. I've usually found it more effective to use my brain.

When I was a boy, I fooled my mother into thinking that the thing I liked most was the thing I didn't care about. I had a bike, which I loved, and a bow and arrow, which I wasn't too wild about. Every time my mother told me to go outside and ride my bike, I made a big deal over the bow and arrow. Then, when I had to be punished, that's the thing she took away. I never lost my riding privileges.

Today, karate is a way for the thinking man. It is a logical, complex art, and to learn it requires discipline, motivation, and self-restraint. The higher your intellect, the better a karateist you can become.

The karateist must rely more upon his brain than his brawn. So you don't need the physique of a Mr. America or an athlete to become accomplished. You can be tall or short, thin or fat, even clumsy at the beginning—it doesn't matter. So if you identify more with the 98-pound weakling than you do with Charles Atlas, don't rule out karate. You can probably become a better karateist than Atlas himself would have been.

Take Will J. He was a real Charles Atlas type. But that didn't make him a good karate student. In fact, Will had some hangups—despite his terrific body.

One day I offered Will a guest pass to hand out to a

friend, who could use it for a free trial lesson. Will refused to take the pass. When I questioned him about it, he admitted that he thought he looked silly in the karate uniform, and he didn't want any of his friends to come to his class and see him. "I don't even want them to know I'm taking karate, period," he said.

"Why not? What's wrong with karate?"

"Nothing, really," Will told me. "It just shows that I'm really not quite as tough and confident as I look. If I were, why would I be taking karate?"

Will's attitude toward himself and toward karate eventually changed. But I wanted to tell you his story so you'd realize that the Mr. America type often is no more self-assured than the average-looking man, someone who doesn't attract huge flocks of women at the beach.

In a way, the less physically developed individual has an advantage over a muscle-bound strong man. A student who has devoted himself to physical culture, who has developed huge muscles, perhaps through weight lifting, probably thinks of strength as relative to the size of his muscles. He thinks that the bigger the muscle, the more weight he can lift, the harder he can hit, the farther he can throw. So before he can learn karate, he has to unlearn his concept of what strength is. In karate, strength depends on speed, flexibility, balance, coordination, endurance, and muscle tone (not size). The muscle-man often neglects developing himself in these other areas.

The student who hasn't worked on developing his physique may be able to learn karate faster because he has less to unlearn. He will be more versatile because of his less developed musculature. While the overdeveloped man has often limited himself to moves involving

weight and power, the underdeveloped student can concentrate on whatever area is most appealing to him:
agility, speed, strategy, or power.

Just as you needn't be a Charles Atlas to become a
good karateist, neither do you have to be a first-rate
athlete. Size means nothing in karate. The small person
is not by definition a weak person. A jockey has the
capacity to be as strong and as fit in the karate sense as
a basketball player. In some ways, the jockey's potential
is even greater because he may be faster and more agile.

More important than a student's size or strength is his
capacity for self-discipline. A good karate student has to
have the ability to exert some control over his actions.
This does not mean that you have to think of yourself
as a self-disciplined person before you begin karate.
Maybe you've wanted to stop smoking and haven't been
able to. You tell yourself you have no self-discipline.
Maybe you've been meaning to do calisthenics for twenty
minutes every morning and after three days you quit.
Don't feel you aren't qualified to learn karate. Discipline
is taught along with the moves in karate, and all you
need is the *capacity* to learn it.

In fact, people who are too disciplined, who have every
thought and action under tight control, are frequently
poor students. Overly disciplined people often lack spirit,
and they find it hard to free themselves of conscious
thought. In karate, we allow our energy to flow directly
from thought to action, without the interference of conscious deliberation. We eliminate a step, to unify thought
and action, to empty the mind so that our energy just
flows naturally. The overly disciplined individual has a
difficult time emptying his mind. He is usually thinking,
pushing, forcing himself into uncomfortable patterns,
patterns of behavior and action that do not come

naturally to him, and at the same time, repressing those that are natural.

The ideal karate student has a vital discipline, a dynamic rather than a robotlike control. He will be able to harness his energy for use more easily than the man who habitually—and unconsciously—keeps it in check.

As important as the capacity for dynamic discipline is the capacity to think intelligently. Karate is attracting students who are involved with their minds as well as their bodies. If karate were only beating up the other guy, these students wouldn't be interested to the extent that they are, and they wouldn't be as good karateists. The intelligent student of the 1970s is a true karateist, not only a self-defense expert. He perceives the strategy behind the moves, the thought behind the action, and he applies this philosophy to every area of his life.

Is there an ideal age to learn karate? Children generally make very good students—children's minds are more open and they learn more easily—although they require very special care and attention. Around age six is as early as they should begin, since most younger children cannot take instruction well enough to learn efficiently.

Karate should not be thought of as an activity exclusively for the strong, well-coordinated, physically capable child. It has as many benefits, if not more, for the awkward, less self-assured youngster. Many physical education teachers recommend karate as an adjunct to the school's physical fitness program, especially for children who are not particularly comfortable expressing themselves physically. It's an excellent means of improving coordination and reflexes and building self-confidence. In addition, of course, it enables a child to protect himself if necessary.

Many parents who enroll their children for self-defense

and physical training reasons discover that karate helps in other ways, too. One parent wrote, several months after her nine-year-old son began karate lessons: "I never dreamed my son would be helped so much. He had been running with a tough group of boys, and because he was the youngest, they sometimes picked on him. I wanted him to be able to fight back, but now he has found a new group of friends entirely. His teachers tell me he applies himself better in his school work and he is no longer a discipline problem.

"Around the house, he is more talkative, less sullen. My husband and I are enjoying him, and we are able to communicate. He complains less about his chores."

Adults become very successful karateists, and not only young adults. Many of the world's finest masters are in their forties and fifties. I knew of one man who began at age sixty and became a famous master at the age of eighty. And he is not an exception.

But you don't have to become a master to benefit from and enjoy karate. You can begin at any age and learn as much as you wish. I have one student who is fifty-five and says, "I have gained so much energy and stamina from karate that I feel better now than I felt ten years ago." Karate may be for you, even if you are a grandfather or a grandmother.

Women can become as successful at karate as men. Some of the world's greatest systems of karate were created by women. Many young women begin karate because of its self-defense aspects and then discover it's a marvelous way to keep trim and fit. Other women study karate as a means of remaining youthful, keeping their muscles toned, and increasing their energy levels. The Chinese *Wu Shu (Kung Fu)* exhibition team has as many women as men.

One of my women students, executive assistant to the president of a famous cosmetics firm, has been taking karate for six months now. She once told me, "Karate has given me a whole new sense of myself. I started just to tone up my body a little, but I've learned an entirely different way of moving and thinking. I find myself more aware of every word I say and every move I make. And for a change, I'm pleased with myself."

So you see, there are no particular physical requirements for the karate student. I've even taught many handicapped people. A handicap need not deter you. Intelligence and the capacity to learn self-discipline are the most important requisites.

Of course, time, money, and motivation must be considered; but these factors play a part in any new activity you might take up. Two evenings a week is ideal if you can spare the time, but one will do. As for the cost, that varies from school to school.

Karate has value for a wide range of people because it fills many different needs—physical, emotional, intellectual, and social. My students come to me from all walks of life, and for many different reasons. For example, I have several doctors who study with me—neurologists, dentists, physiologists, psychologists—men interested in a more intimate understanding of the interaction between mind and body.

A neurologist who has been studying with me for a year is particularly enthusiastic about the degree of control a karateist can exert over his own body systems. He wants to learn more about the mental control of nervous impulses and investigate the potential of treating certain nerve ailments by means of mental training of the karate variety.

Among my students are two priests, who feel that

karate helps them keep in touch with people and sharpens their ability to read people's emotions and needs. "Many people think of priests as being out of the mainstream, out of touch," one of them told me. "But the contacts I've had with people through my karate class have taught me some valuable lessons about humanity and have made me feel less distant from others."

I also have a number of policemen who are studying karate with me because their force doesn't offer karate training. "My karate keeps me sharp, both physically and mentally," said one patrolman. "I spend the whole day in a patrol car, and I tend to get lax. I was losing my muscle tone, and feeling tired a lot of the time before I started karate. Now, after three months, I'm in good condition, and my weight is under control. I feel much better equipped to do my job."

Bus and truck drivers come so they won't lose their muscle tone, energy, and mental alertness in the tedium of driving all day long. A bus driver for fifteen years began studying karate about six months ago. "Outside of feeling generally more fit," he says, "my reaction time is quicker, and that's important when you're driving. I seem to see better, to notice things more, like what the other guy on the road is thinking.

"A few weeks ago I had a close call, and I'll bet a hundred to one I'd have had an accident if I hadn't been as alert as I was. I give karate the credit. I never feel like falling asleep at the wheel anymore, and it takes much less effort to get through the day."

Most schools are filled with students from all walks of life. I have taught everybody from manual laborers to college professors. I've had politicians, nurses, airline pilots and stewardesses, receptionists, computer programmers, antique dealers, mechanics, corporate presidents, salesmen, personnel managers.

One national sales manager for a large electronics firm told me he signed up "because it looked like fun. And I do enjoy it. But it has also taught me so much about dealing with other people, things that have helped me in my work. I now consider it an essential element in my life."

Karate has something to offer to nearly everyone. Anyone who is in reasonably good health can do it. If you enjoy physical well-being, the confidence that comes with self-knowledge, and contact with other intelligent, perceptive, hard-working individuals, then you will enjoy karate.

Chapter 2
What Karate Really Is

Most people have a lot of misconceptions about karate. Some think it is a synonym for violence; others believe karate is magic, that its practitioners have supernatural abilities; some people consider it a sport and attend exhibitions just as they would attend football or hockey games; still others think of it solely as a self-defense technique. Actually, karate is none of these things. Yet, in an odd way, it is all of them.

Real karate is not the violent art you see in the movies. A true karateist never initiates violence but is prepared to respond to attack with violence, if necessary. A major part of a karateist's training is how to avoid violence; and genuine karate encounters, when they do occur, are very brief. They rarely last as long as a full minute, and they bear little resemblance to the lengthy staged combat you see in the movies.

I remember the first time I went into a karate school to observe a class. I thought I was going to see a fantastic show. A couple of people in white uniforms with black belts were on the training floor, and it looked like they were going to fight. I watched them and watched them, but nothing happened. They just seemed to be staring at each other. I turned to my companion and asked him, "What are they waiting for?" By the time I turned back to look at the karateists, one of them was lying on the floor. The whole fight was over, and I'd missed it.

Karate is based on the natural abilities of man, abilities we all possess, all developed to their highest potential. Nevertheless, people persist in thinking there's something magical about it. Even some students, when they first begin karate training, think I have a superpower I'm going to share with them.

You've probably seen karate-type exhibitions on TV, where people break boards or blocks of ice with their bare hands and demonstrate other feats that seem to require superhuman strength. Sometimes people come to my school and ask me how many years it will take them to become that strong. When I tell them I can have them breaking boards with their bare hands in a week or two, they're flabbergasted.

They don't understand that they won't need anything like superhuman strength to break a board. Actually, board-breaking is a simple trick that nearly anyone can master in a very short time. It has little to do with the art and philosophy of karate.

Sport or Weapon?

Karate is not a repertoire of fancy tricks. Neither is it a sport, although people often wrongly think of it as one. Karate is a serious endeavor, with deep meaning for those who practice it. Karateists cannot easily engage in their art for the sake of sport or to entertain. It is too lethal a game. Unlike prize fighting, wrestling, football, hockey and the like, karate does not provide a convenient arena for relatively harmless contests.

That's not to say some people aren't attempting to make it into a sport. I've seen at least four different variations suggested or actually tried.

1. Full-contact karate, in which two (or more) karateists go at each other with no holds barred.
2. Limited-contact karate, in which certain moves are legal, but others are not permitted. This is certainly safer than full-contact karate.
3. "Armored" karate, in which the participants wear protective gear of some sort or gloves. This is safer yet.
4. No-contact karate, in which participants are not allowed to touch or are not allowed ot do each other harm. I favor this method. It preserves the look and philosophy of karate and maintains all the benefits of full contact.

Many people first come to karate to learn self-defense. They end up discovering, to their great surprise, that they have learned a profound philosophy of life that will serve them well—even if they're never threatened with physical harm.

Publicity vs. Reality

Karate is very complex, and people misunderstand it for a lot of reasons. Television and movies certainly haven't portrayed karate accurately. What you've read in most books and magazine articles hasn't brought you any closer to the truth. The media misrepresent karate by emphasizing its more spectacular, bizarre, and lethal aspects. Sensationalism in movies means big box office. In TV shows it means high ratings. In books it means best-sellers, and in magazines it means high circulation. The media have nothing to gain by focusing on the gentler, philosophical aspects of karate. So one reason you probably don't know much about how karate can be of value to you (other than as a means of self-defense) is because nobody's ever bothered to tell you, or show you.

The art of karate has been shrouded in secrecy ever since its beginnings. The earliest karateists used their art to protect themselves against their enemies, and they guarded their knowledge as if they had some special secret. Very little detailed information about the martial arts was ever written down, and artistic representations of karate were deliberately ambiguous and misleading. The karateists of long ago took painstaking care to confine the knowledge—both the self-defense and the philosophy—not only to their own groups, but to the worthiest members within the group. They feared that the art would become misused, diluted, or otherwise abused if it fell into the wrong hands. Nevertheless, despite the continuing secrecy, the arts did spread and develop throughout Asia.

In the United States, this secrecy has given birth to a mystique. It's not easy to break completely with the past, and I'm not advocating that. But karate in the United States is still laden with Oriental languages, customs, and costumes which go far beyond the simple and appropriate honoring of tradition.

Excessive worship of the past disturbs me because it masks the true nature of the art. It makes karate seem unfamiliar and unapproachable when, really, the opposite is true. It makes the art seem more Oriental than universal, and universal it is, as you will see. All in all, this mystique, by promoting a closed-shop atmosphere, tends to keep karate exclusive and discourages its natural spread.

Historical Wellsprings

Most authorities believe that karate—or, rather, its ancient precursor—was originated by a man named Bodhidharma (or Ta Mo, or Daruma), who was also the originator of Zen Buddhism. He was an Indian monk who arrived in China around A.D. 520 after crossing the Himalayas on foot.

Once in China, Bodhidharma began to spread his religious philosophy. He became a teacher with many disciples. To his consternation, he found that many of his students were so frail and ill-conditioned that they had trouble staying awake during meditation. Furthermore, they were defenseless if attacked by robbers. To remedy this weakness, and to bring his disciples closer to their souls, Bodhidharma gave them a set of eighteen movements—calisthenics in a way—to perform faithfully every morning. Eventually, these movements and their accompanying philosophies developed into the various martial arts.

Bodhidharma was schooled in the wisdom of ancient India, and his contemporaries in China had an even more ancient culture all their own. So some of the major influences that helped shape karate really predated Bodhidharma by thousands of years. They were:

1. *Ancient Indian and Chinese fighting arts.* According to some sources, Bodhidharma was a member of India's warrior caste (a group of people similar to the Japanese samurai and the medieval knights of Europe). If so, he was a student of *nata*, a dancelike martial art, and *vajramushti*, a martial art that used the fist as a weapon. Both predate the birth of Christ by at least three thousand years.

Many ancient Indian Buddhist statues include figures posed in karatelike stances. This is also true of some ancient Buddhist statues in the temples of Japan. Sometimes the figures portray exact karate postures.

If Bodhidharma did bring these ideas to China, a reasonable assumption, he found there a precursor of karate called, among other things, *chi-chi* ("adroit striking"). Some authorities believe weaponless forms of combat in China date back to the days of Huang Ti, the "Yellow Emperor," whose army evidently used them in battle as long ago as 2674 B.C. But these ancient fighting systems were only part of what went into Bodhidharma's formulation.

2. *Buddhism and its nonviolent philosophy.* The early Buddhist monks in India were pacifists and were forbidden by Buddhist law to harm any other living things. But Buddhism was not a dogmatic religion. One of its main principles was toleration of other beliefs, so

Buddhism was able to change through the ages. As the religion spread throughout China, monks who wanted to train for combat were not ejected from the temples. They were allowed to learn to fight and use weapons, but only on the condition that they followed the Buddhist edict; to fight only when there was no other recourse, and to use their martial skills only for self-defense.

3. *Yoga, its exercises and movements.* The principles of yoga developed within the Hindu religion, which began in northern India about thirty-five hundred years ago. As a Buddhist monk many centuries later, Bodhidharma was undoubtedly familiar with yoga, since Buddhism itself began as an outgrowth of Hinduism in the sixth century B.C.

The main goal of yoga is spiritual development, but the yogis believe that this development cannot be achieved without first mastering the body. So in yoga, one learns to exercise before learning to meditate. Yoga exercises benefit both the muscular system and the body's internal organs. We can see many of yoga's slow motion forms in the martial arts today.

4. *Taoism and its respiratory techniques.* The first writings in the Chinese religion of Taoism were recorded by the historian Lao Tzu in the sixth century B.C., about the same time that Buddhism was spreading throughout India.

The basic Taoist concepts concern the way the universe functions, the path taken by natural events. It is marked by spontaneous creativity and regular changes. A key Taoist idea speaks of effortless action, as in the flowing of water, which unresistingly goes to the lowest level yet wears away rock and stone. The Taoist universe is continuous, ever-flowing, ever-changing, taking the path of least resistance.

Buddhism and Taoism began to blend in China during the first two centuries A.D., but it was not until Bodhidharma came to China in the sixth century that the mixture took on its own identity—Zen Buddhism.

The Taoist meditators began their rituals with deep in-and-out breathing exercises designed to release energy and stimulate circulation. Breath control, you'll discover as you read on, is a major element in karate training and practice. The Taoist learned about breathing in part from animals.

5. *Animals.* The ancients always studied nature carefully. Since animals were a major part of the environment, men studied them exhaustively, hoping to learn something about man's own nature in the process. In developing exercises for self-improvement, self-defense, and health, Asian masters from most of the schools imitated the animals' movements and patterned their forms after them. But for many masters, the study of animal movements was secondary to the study of their emotions and responses to the environment.

When these masters observed the animals' behavior, they discovered some things that amazed them. They learned that animals could be incredibly strong in some circumstances yet not so strong in others. They discovered that animal senses functioned particularly well in certain situations but not so efficiently at other times, depending on need.

They came to realize that animals responded automatically, effortlessly, and with peak efficiency to whatever situation arose. Unlike man, they did not stop to consider their actions. Their responses were not interrupted by conscious thought; their senses were perfectly developed; they were truly in harmony with their environment and at one with themselves.

Striving for a harmony and unity of their own, the masters made an important observation about the animals: the natural flow of emotion and the unrestricted flow of focused energy occurred simultaneously—and were controlled by the way the animals breathed.

6. *The* I Ching *and its principle of harmonizing with change.* The *I Ching,* or Chinese *Book of Changes,* is one of the oldest written works in existence. It was, and is, used by fortune-tellers to predict the future and to give advice. In ancient days it was studied by all learned Chinese, who used it as a guide to gain self-awareness and to gain perspective about themselves in relation to their environment.

The core idea of the *I Ching* is that the world and all within it are at once changeless and always changing. In fact, the Chinese character for "I" represents both change and changelessness. The character derives from the ideograms for "sun" and "moon," which are both ever-changing (they rise and set every day) and changeless (they are always in the heavens).

To relate to this world of changing/changelessness, the individual must (according to the *I Ching*) harmonize and move with the change, redirecting it if necessary, rather than by resisting with force. At the same time, the individual must maintain his equilibrium and clear sense of self.

7. *The concept of* yin *and* yang. The principle of the *yin* and *yang,* upon which the *I Ching* is based, dates back nearly five thousand years. Its best-known interpreter was the Taoist historian Lao Tzu.

The *yin* and *yang* symbolize the polarities that exist everywhere in nature: male/female, dark/bright, moon/ sun, soft/hard, weak/strong, environment/self, receive/

respond, mind/body, conscious/unconscious, positive/negative—there's no end to the list you can make.

The *yin/yang* symbol above illustrates the concept. You can see that the *yin* and the *yang* are each incomplete without the other. They are opposites, but they are not independent. Rather, they lean on each other for their existence. They cannot be totally separated because of their dual nature—an idea represented by the dark speck of *yang* within the white *yin* and the spot of *yin* within the *yang*. Nothing in nature, says this principle, is all one thing or all the other. Everything includes its opposite to some extent.

The martial arts were inspired and influenced mainly by these seven ideas. Books have been written on each subject. But this brief background will help you understand how they're connected to karate. You can think of the martial arts as extensions of these ideas—physical applications of ancient Indian and Chinese thought.

New Names and Old

The martial art that Bodhidharma developed, Shaolin Temple boxing, was also called *Chun Kuo ch'uan* ("Chinese fist"), *Ch'uan shu*, and *Ch'uan fa*. As the arts began to evolve further and spread within China, they became known collectively as *kung fu*. Actually, *kung fu* translates into "master" (*kung*) and "man" (*fu*). So *kung fu* means "master of man," in the sense of "master of self." People who practiced *kung fu* were attempting to better themselves through a self-improvement program.

As time passed, other forms of *kung fu* popped up throughout the rest of Asia, evolving on their own to meet a specific need or through knowledge brought by Chinese traders and diplomats. The differences among these arts—inevitable cultural adaptations—were relatively minor and not nearly as significant as the fact that they all more or less adhered to Bodhidharma's teachings.

The word "karate" is not only a generic term like *kung fu*, but also refers to a specific martial art that developed in Okinawa in the seventeenth century as a direct outgrowth of Japanese subjugation of that island and the prohibition of weapons there. But it wasn't called karate until the twentieth century. That name was chosen with great care, not only because the word karate reflects the Chinese, Japanese, and Okinawan background of the art, but because it also symbolizes the philosophic values common to all the martial arts.

Most people wrongly think that the word karate, which literally means "empty hand" (*kara te*), refers to the weaponless aspects of the art. Actually, the Okinawans developed clandestine weapons as they were perfecting the art. Earlier martial arts forms in China and those that developed elsewhere in Asia also used weapons from time to time.

Karate is really an idiomatic expression that you can't interpret literally any more than you can literally interpret the phrase "raining cats and dogs." *Kara* and *te* are linked and juxtaposed opposites just like *yin* and *yang*, with *kara* embodying the *yin* (soft, weak, female, etc.) and *te* embodying the *yang* (hard, strong, male, etc.).

The symbol used for *kara* refers to an empty mind—one that reflects clearly, and is unhampered by the intrusion of conscious thought—or to an open, receptive mind—one whose vision is not distorted by preconceived ideas. *Te,* or fist, is based on the symbol for determination, for commitment, for strict adherence to a hard line. It is the opposite of *kara.* *Te* is unchanging, *kara* is change; *te* is self, *kara* is other; *te* is sending, *kara* is receiving; *te* is action, *kara* reaction.

Principles of Karate

Over the centuries, all the concepts interacting with the cultures they came from produced literally hundreds of martial arts systems, which we're grouping here under the name karate. Nearly all the systems have at their heart similar philosophical principles that can be applied to all aspects of life: physical health, psychological stability, success in business, self-protection, rewarding relationships with others, intellectual growth, and emotional satisfaction. These principles are not only interrelated and intertwined, but in many ways contained in each other. For the sake of clarity, let's consider them separately.

Discipline. What does the word discipline mean to you? willpower? self-control? punishment or denial? inflexibility? rigid routine? You probably have lots of associations with the idea of discipline, and I'm willing to bet most of them are negative. If you're like most people, you think that discipline prevents spontaneity and dampens the human "spirit." At best, it's a necessary evil. I know a few people who use this notion as an excuse for not disciplining themselves or their children.

The truth of the matter is, they think discipline is difficult if not impossible to achieve. Really, it isn't.

It just requires commitment and determination and pays off handsomely. Wisely and properly applied, discipline —in the karate sense—doesn't kill "spirit." Quite the contrary. Discipline helps to create order, and an individual who feels "in order" also feels free and capable— free enough to release his energy spontaneously and capable of controlling its intensity and direction to suit his purpose, whatever it may be.

Karate itself is a discipline—that is, a body of knowledge that must be handed down from teacher to student. The karateist begins his studies by learning to discipline his body to do what it's told. This leads to discipline of the mind, development of strong character and self-control, not as repression of self, but as mastery of self. The karateist's discipline does not tie him down, but enables him to use what he has to get what he wants.

Adaptability. Whether you know it or not, you are constantly changing. Even if you look the same, act the same, think the same, and feel the same as you did a year ago—or yesterday—you're different now. You're not even the same from one minute to the next—not completely—because biochemical and electrical changes are occurring within you each fraction of a second. When those changes stop, when all is still inside you, life is over.

The world you live in today isn't the same world you lived in a year ago, or yesterday—any more than you are the same person now that you were then. Even if everything seems the same—your house, your car, your job— they aren't. Certainly things outside your immediate environment have changed too. You can tell simply by comparing the newspaper from a year ago—or yesterday's paper—to the one that landed on your doorstep this morning.

So you and your environment are always in a state of flux, always changing, even when you can't perceive the change. The very air you breathe changes from moment to moment. Its molecules are in constant motion. The air around you is always moving, circulating, making a fresh supply of oxygen available so you can live.

The point I'm making is this: change, at every level of life, is necessary for the continuance of life; because this is so, willingness and ability to adapt to change are requisites for living. The greater the adaptability, the better (and longer) the life. Adaptability itself is a kind of change, a shift you make in response to other shifts inside you or in your environment.

In karate, adapting to change doesn't mean the same thing as adjusting to it, resigning yourself to it, conforming to it, or accommodating yourself to it. These responses all suggest a denial of self, a surrender to change. But change—even unpleasant change—is such a vital part of life that it can't be considered an enemy. We don't have to surrender ourselves to change any more than we have to fight it.

In karate, you learn to feel comfortable with the basic idea of change. More than that, you learn how to make change a friend to rely on and use. Of course, you can't do this if you're overwhelmed by change, so karate-adaptability teaches you to keep your wits and your balance, to maintain your sense of self, not to get lost or swept away—even during your most vulnerable moments: in the midst of chaotic change (or any change) and at the instant you are shifting in response to that change.

The principle of adaptability is closely related to— really inseparable from—three other concepts that have their origins in the *I Ching*: harmonization with change and redirection of force, dynamic balance, and the duality of nature. These concepts themselves are interrelated and nearly inseparable from one another. They are also very abstract. But please bear with me, even if you can't imagine how to apply them to your own situation. I'll give you plenty of examples when I discuss self-defense and other benefits of karate later in the book.

1. *Harmonization with change and redirection of force.* Responding to change karate-style means blending in with change, becoming one with it, moving with it. Once we are moving with change, we are in a unique position. We can either let ourselves be carried along by the force of the change in a direction that seems beneficial or interesting, or we can alter or redirect that force onto a course that's better suited to our needs.

Whether we ride on the force or whether we rechannel it, we are *using* it. Either we rely totally on the momentum of the change, preserving our own energy and strength; or we augment our own energy and strength with the force and momentum of the change.

2. *Dynamic balance.* Most people, as they go through life, are either in a state of balance or imbalance at any given moment. When we are in balance—physically or mentally—we are standing still. Our position is fixed, certain, and secure. But when we begin to move (as we must if we are to respond to our environment) we lose our balance, our certainty, and our security—for however long it takes us to get back to our fixed position or to arrive at a new one.

Karate teaches us to achieve a state of dynamic balance in which we come extremely close to being simultaneously in balance and in motion. So we aren't very likely to be thrown off balance—to stumble or become confused—in our dealings with ourselves and the rest of the world. We're also better prepared to harmonize with change and put it to work for us.

By retaining our equilibrium, we are at once shifting and stable. We are microcosms of the universe, which is also simultaneously shifting and stable, moving and unmoving, changing and changeless (in the *yin/yang* sense).

3. *Duality of nature.* The ancient idea of the duality of the universe and the individual within lies behind all karate thought. It's what makes karate philosophy so practical and so timeless.

Karate expresses its own dual nature by calling itself "the art of the soft and the hard." On one level, this concept is expressed in the notion of dynamic balance, which encourages and enables you to be at once soft (shifting, moving, responding) and hard (balanced, stable, secure). Karate itself has adapted through the ages by being soft (changing to fit the people's needs) and hard (sticking to the principles on which it was originally founded).

Actually, the very idea of adapting to change is "soft" —harmonizing as opposed to resisting, which is "hard." So adaptability, as a principle of karate is based on the belief that things which are soft, pliable, and in motion are really far more powerful than things which are hard, rigid, and unmoving—that the soft way is a far more effective way of dealing with change and is a far more efficient way to affect change. There are many simple demonstrations in nature of the power of the soft. Take water (soft) and stone (hard). The gently flowing water in a brook will eventually erode the rocks at its bottom, no matter how hard they are.

On a deeper level, the concept of soft/hard is also at the core of the next principle:

Nonconfrontation. The idea of nonconfrontation pervades a karateist's thinking and influences his entire pattern of behavior. I've already shown you how the nonconfrontation principle governs the principle of adaptability: harmonizing with change rather than confronting it with resistance. And I'll show you in the self-defense chapter how the principle prevents violence.

Nonconfrontation is a predominantly soft approach to life, which a karateist uses whenever possible. Some people have difficulty believing in the validity of that approach. Maybe you're one of them. You may have grown up hearing over and over phrases like rise to every challenge, meet the opposition head on, don't let anyone step on your toes, beat the other guy to the punch, fight fire with fire, stand your ground, stick up for your rights, and so on. The lesson in these phrases is circular: I'd better not appear weak. If I do, people will try to take advantage of me. If I let people take advantage of me, I'll appear weak.

And so we learn to approach life "hard." As hard as we can, to keep from being hurt or to prove to ourselves and others that we're worthy. The hard approach to life can be pretty unfriendly. It takes many different forms, of course, and occurs in varying degrees. Sometimes we're hostile, untrusting, aggressive, or rigid. Sometimes we create conflict. Sometimes we merely welcome it. But we rarely pass up an opportunity to confront. We think that willingness to confront makes us look strong, even if we don't come out top dog every time. We think avoiding conflict is a sign of weakness. Whatever we learned about how "bad" it is to be soft or weak—and however well we learned to pretend to be hard and strong—we didn't learn much, if anything, about really being strong.

Karate teaches us the true nature of confrontation and the true nature of strength. We learn there's no shame in appearing weak. We learn we don't need to confront to feel or appear strong. Confrontation gives us only a false sense of security at best. In karate, we acquire self-confidence in many different areas, and we can approach life softly because we know we can be hard when we have to. We also know, as I mentioned when discussing adaptability, that the softer way is usually the more powerful, even though it may not seem so to the uninitiated.

But simply believing in the soft way isn't all it takes to live according to the principle of nonconfrontation. That takes discipline and awareness. It is through our discipline that we learn to be strong, and it is through our discipline that we become aware.

Awareness lets us see the place of the soft approach and lets us feel secure enough to rely on it. We can use our awareness to find clever ways to avoid confrontation. And just as important, we can use it to know when confrontation is inevitable. With awareness, we learn to use the hard approach only when circumstances permit no other alternative.

Awareness is a word nearly everyone throws around these days, without bothering to define it. What do I mean by awareness? I mean knowledge. Self-knowledge and knowledge of the environment, which is always increased by knowledge of self. Self-knowledge is vital to achieving a state of dynamic balance. Awareness of the environment is crucial to perceiving change, and so to adapting. Awareness makes it possible to rid ourselves of preconceptions that inhibit adaptability and growth. Awareness creates the climate for unlimited self-development. It gives us better control over our own lives.

How the Principles Are Taught

The first martial artists learned their art from the "inside out." They devoted themselves to intellectual and meditative pursuits before learning the physical discipline. But this was merely a matter of practicality and culture.

If you're like most Americans, you're a little impatient, you want action. You're going to appreciate the fact that karate can be taught just as well from the outside in as it can from the inside out. Most Americans have learned karate from the outside in, and they are in no way inferior to their Oriental counterparts.

We begin from the outside by first becoming aware of our bodies. Karate teaches us to develop and discipline our bodies to make them able to respond to our commands.

Karate routines—also called *katas*—are not really exercises in the calisthenic sense. They may be more accurately described as choreographed movements, or forms. Depending on the system of karate you're studying, you may have anywhere from one to fifty *katas* to learn.

You won't have much difficulty learning them—at least superficially. At first, you'll probably have trouble believing how something that seems so simple can so profoundly affect you. But learning the *katas* is like learning the letters of the alphabet. Eventually, you'll be using those letters to read and write. Eventually, you'll be learning the lessons of the *katas* in every aspect of your life. This will become clear as you practice the *katas* over and over, mastering them on several different levels.

In the beginning, we learn to perform the shortest, least complicated *katas*, and we learn to execute them slowly. The emphasis is on precision. Remember, you are educating your body through the *katas*, teaching it to do exactly what you tell it. Later, we learn the longer, more complex *katas*. We practice increasing our speed without losing our precision. We also learn to vary the intensity with which we perform the *katas*. As beginners, we practice the routines alone, without a partner. But as soon as we become somewhat accomplished—and this happens rather quickly—we can advance to sparring with a partner, and engage in actual physical contact.

From the first moment we begin learning the *katas*, we are putting into practice with our physical being the principles of karate. As we progress, the *katas* take on new meanings, as do the principles themselves. Once we acquire some initial discipline and begin to work with a partner, we start learning what adaptability really is. We have to relate our own movements to those of another individual. We begin to comprehend the nature of change, the meaning of harmonization with change and redirection of force, the feeling of dynamic balance and the differences between soft and hard. By enacting various situations of confrontation through the *katas*, we begin to comprehend the nature of conflict, and we begin to learn how and when we can avoid it and what to do when we can't.

As your mastery of the *katas* builds, you will come to see how you are expressing the basic karate principles and philosophy spontaneously through your body movements, which have become smooth and automatic. You will notice that your mind no longer has to tell your body what to do. Your mind and your body are functioning as one. You begin to feel more "together," and whatever internal conflicts you may have become less strong and wrenching. The initial bodily awareness and discipline you acquire through the *katas* will now begin to generalize through your entire being. You will move toward a deeper, more complete self-knowledge and self-control.

By this time, you will find you're beginning to internalize the lessons of the *katas*. The karate principles are becoming an integral part of you. You start to express them not only through your body in karate class, but also with your whole self, wherever you are, whatever you do. You are making karate truly your own. And the most profound part of this process—this journey from outside to in—is that it occurs automatically, without conscious effort. It is the natural, inevitable result of learning the *katas*.

As I write this, I am painfully aware that this truth—and I know it to be a truth from my own experience—cannot be convincingly conveyed by anything but the actual experience of it. But believe me, it is so.

What Karate Is Here and Now

Now that you know what karate isn't, where it came from, what its basic principles are and how they're taught, you're also ready to hear what karate has become today:

   1. *The perfect exercise.* At its simplest level, karate provides the body with total exercise for both musculature and internal systems.

2. *The path to good physical health.* Karate not only makes your body fit. It actually helps cure some diseases and makes you more resistant to others.

3. *The best means of self-defense known to man.* Karate isn't a way to violence, but a way to avoid violence if possible and handle it if you can't.

4. *The path to good mental health.* Karate makes you stronger intellectually and emotionally, helps you behave less neurotically. Karate doesn't make you conform to society's mold, but it does help you function effectively within society.

5. *The way to superalertness.* You can't very well adapt to your environment if you're slow to perceive and react to what's happening around you. Karate develops your senses and sharpens your reflexes.

6. *A way to thrive on stress.* Stress, properly handled, need not endanger your life. You don't have to avoid stress in order to avoid its harmful effects. Karate teaches you how to deal with stress, to use it productively and safely.

7. *A way to become a unified person.* Karate liberates your energy and frees your spirit. It enables you to harness the power of your mind to the power of your body and direct that combined energy to achieve your goals. It leads you to function as a unified being, without consciously working against yourself.

8. *A philosophy of life.* Karate offers you a set of values in an age that suffers from lack of them. It doesn't give you rigid rules, but rather flexible, practical principles you can use to guide your life regardless of your circumstances.

9. *A road to self-discovery.* Through karate, you gain awareness and self-knowledge. You don't go through life with vague yearnings, failing to get what you want because you can't define it.

10. *A way to realize your full potential.* Karate teaches you not to assume false limitations of your own capabilities. As a karateist, you won't tell yourself you can't do something just because you never did it before. Quite the contrary. With karate, you will find yourself accomplishing things you previously imagined were impossible.

11. *A road to self-fulfillment.* As a self-improvement program, karate makes all the others seem haphazard and incomplete. It is the one discipline, the one art, that can teach you how to magnify your own abilities many times over. With karate you can function at peak efficiency, deriving maximum pleasure and satisfaction out of life.

If you are willing to make the commitment, karate can improve the way you think, the way you look, the way you act, the way you deal with your environment, your relations with other people, how you perform on the job, your ability to plan for the future. It can improve the inner you and the outer you. The whole you.

Chapter 3

Becoming a Whole Person

The principal aim of karate is nothing less than to make its practitioners into complete, fully realized human beings, both mentally and physically—people who can call forth all their resources and use their total capabilities at will.

Few people attain that state naturally. Left to our own ends, most of us respond to life's demands in a fragmented fashion. We seldom, if ever, are truly able to give our all—even when nothing less will do. Instead of reacting to the challenges of everyday life by focusing and directing our energies to the task at hand, we respond haphazardly and incompletely. Instead of giving our best, we try to get by with giving "enough" (which it rarely is).

We deal with life's demands inefficiently most of the time. We tire more quickly than we should. We get distracted too easily. We frequently get confused. We try "too hard." What we almost never do is live up to our full potential.

When our daily challenges go beyond the ordinary, when we get ourselves into emergency situations with extraordinary work loads, deadlines, high-tension confrontations, or unusual physical demands, we do even worse. Sometimes we choke up and fail. We freeze. Yet we know we could handle such situations quite easily, if only we could put our full capacities to work. We know we're using only a fraction of our abilities. We know that if we could put everything we had to work for us, we could be far more successful, far happier, far more satisfied with our lives.

In fact, a strong case could be made for the notion that the most successful people, the happiest people, the people most satisfied with their lives are those who have somehow found a way to use a greater percentage of their natural talents and abilities than the rest of us.

I'm not berating anyone for laziness, lack of determination, or a weak character. The problem I'm talking about goes far deeper than that. It involves the way people view themselves. The plain fact is that most of us don't see ourselves as unified human beings. We make a separation between our minds—our intellects and our emotions—and our bodies. Most of us are like Jekyll and Hyde. Sometimes we downgrade the importance of our bodies, seeing our physical selves only as machines to serve and be directed by our mental selves, our *real* selves. Other times, we block off the mind, repressing or ignoring emotions that are disturbing or inconvenient. Some of us, instead of oscillating back and forth between favoring the mind and the body, settle on one part and develop and emphasize it at the expense of the other part. Some even develop a part of a part—the intellect vs. the emotions, for instance.

Yet any separation we make, any division of self, is artificial, not natural. The brain, after all, is a *physical* entity. Even our thoughts are physical in nature, electrical impulses traveling along nerve pathways. Without the body, there would be no such thing as a mind. For that matter, without the mind there would be no such thing as the body. The things we think of as strictly physical— movement, coordination, perception of sensation, natural bodily functions—are actually mental. Bodily circumstances—pain, hunger, fever, injury—affect the mind. Mental circumstances—worry, joy, shock, excitement— affect the body. A bodily illness can adversely affect the mind, and a mental illness can adversely affect the body.

There is nothing we can do, of course, to break this link. It exists whether or not we acknowledge it. But, over the centuries, because of the demands of civilization and through evolution, humanity has forged a barrier between the two selves. This barrier prevents us from being whole, unified, integrated human beings. This barrier prevents us from giving our best when we're confronted with the challenges of everyday life. And it is this barrier that karate seeks to transcend.

Let's take a closer look at these challenges and demands and how we meet them and see why we inevitably give less than our best as long as we cannot overcome the barrier between mind and body.

Stress and Energy

To a greater or lesser degree, all stimuli—everything that happens to us—create a stress reaction. Our muscles tense, our blood pressure goes up, our blood sugar increases, our adrenalin flows, our nerve endings become more sensitive, we breathe faster, we sweat.

In the words of psychologist Walter B. Cannon, we have a "fight or flight" reaction when confronted with stimuli. We go into fast idle, trying to get ready for anything. And this happens whether the stimulus is unpleasant—a threat, for instance—or pleasant—a phone call about winning the state lottery. We perceive stimuli as stress. This stress creates or liberates what the Orientals call *chi*, or *ki*, and what Westerners refer to as energy, vital force, nervous energy, psychic energy, vitality, vim and vigor, sparkle, the inner spirit, the life force, and so on.

Even in ancient days, the Orientals operated on the basis that *chi* was not just a poetic idea, but that such energy actually existed, that it flowed through the body and was used to power all mental and physical activities. Only recently, however, has anyone come up with any scientific evidence backing the existence of such a force. This evidence appears in what are known as Kirlian photographs, images created by the direct contact between film and the object being "photographed."

These images show what appear to be patterns of electrical discharge emanating from living things—the fingers and toes of human beings, the stems and leaves of plants, etc. These patterns are not always the same. When a person is angry, for example, the discharges emanating from his fingertips are more visible and have a deeper color, usually red. When a person is quiet and thoughtful, the discharges are minimal and usually blue.

This, of course, is right in line with the ancients' thinking about *chi*. As they saw it, this force ebbed and flowed according to mood and need. And the Kirlian photographs also fit the theory that *chi* is produced by or stimulated by stress. The stronger the stress, the stronger the discharge.

It even seems right that the *chi*—if that's what it is— shows up in Kirlian photographs in an apparently electrical form. The Orientals have long believed *chi* and electricity were related, which in and of itself is interesting, since we know that the messages sent along the nerves are nothing more than minute electrical impulses.

Chi is the product of stress. And the more intense the stress, the more *chi* is liberated for use. The more energy, or *chi*, a man needs, the more he will have— assuming all systems are functioning properly. This is a natural, normal phenomenon. There's nothing strange or mystical about it.

These days, it's very popular to blame stress for many, if not most problems. Various authorities have said it can cause high blood pressure, ulcers, mental breakdowns, and all sorts of other difficulties. There's no way— fortunately—to get rid of stress. It is the inevitable result of any change. The only way to get rid of stress is to lock yourself in a box. Even then, you'll feel stress wondering if your meal is going to be slipped through the slot punctually.

Stress is neither good nor bad. It's what you do with it that counts. If you let it produce *chi*, and you find a good outlet for that *chi*, then the more stress you experience, the more vital a person you'll be. If you use the *chi* it stimulates to repress stress, however, you're in trouble.

As far as I'm concerned, tranquilizers are taking the wrong tack in regard to stress. They work to make you immune to stress. Tranquilizers dull your perception of stress and reduce your physiological reactions to it. But they also prevent you from experiencing the benefits of stress. They diminish your vitality and your energy. They numb you and keep you quiet.

By reducing your reaction to stress, tranquilizers also reduce the amount of *chi* a person has at his disposal. I suppose that for severe neurotics, who bottle up this energy and use it to magnify their anxiety, fear, depression, or whatever, this may have some value. But for the rest of us—the great majority of us—to ignore the reality of stress may reduce our capacity to deal with life's problems, to enjoy life's pleasures, to live with the intensity with which we're capable, to be alive and vital.

Incidentally, this view of stress isn't limited to karateists like myself. One of the world's greatest authorities on the subject, Dr. Hans Seyle, author of *Stress Without Distress* (New York: Lippincott, 1974), also believes that stress can have a very positive value in our lives.

We're dealing with complex concepts here—the unity (or disunity) of mind and body, the meaning of stress, the force that gives us life and vitality (*chi*). So let's step out of the abstract for a moment to see how they might all come together in real life.

Let's imagine, for a moment, how stress and *chi* would interact in a person who is totally unified, who has no artificial barriers between mind and body. Such a man would be a master karateist in my view, even if he's never heard of the martial arts.

Let's say, for example, that this man is driving along a highway when his left front tire suddenly blows out. The result would doubtless be instant stress, instant stress reaction, and instant stimulation of *chi*—plenty of it.

Our unified man—operating without conscious thought —would take his *chi* and use every last bit of it to deal with the emergency he's facing. Whether or not he'd succeed depends on the circumstances. But he wouldn't defeat himself. He'd keep a cool head, he wouldn't panic. He'd react as quickly as it's possible for him to react. He'd utilize *all* his arm strength to keep the car on the road, in a controlled manner. His perceptions and judgment would be at their peak as he considered all the relevant factors—weather, traffic, speed, obstacles, etc.

Now let's put the average individual in that same car— a man who is no more or less unified than most people. How would he behave?

Well, his experience would begin more or less the same way. Once he realized what was happening—and he probably wouldn't grasp the situation as quickly as the unified man, who'd be more alert and aware—he, too, would have instant stress, instant stress reaction, and instant stimulation of *chi*, and in the same amount as his unified counterpart. But there the resemblance would end. Our un-unified man might freeze or panic. He would react more slowly, less surely. His muscle strength might diminish. Even if it didn't, he probably wouldn't be able to control it precisely. His perception and judgment would be considerably clouded by his shock and panic.

In all, our un-unified man would perform less well in this emergency than he would under normal conditions. And his chances of surviving the episode would be much smaller than those of his unified counterpart. If he did come through the experience unscathed, he'd feel drained and exhausted. His opposite number would feel exhilarated and energized.

What I'm saying here is that for most of us, *chi*, or energy, is not a force we can control and use to our best advantage. Usually we waste a great deal of it unproductively, or we use part of it on behalf of our objectives and—without realizing it, without intending to—part of it against those same objectives. In an emergency, for instance, we should be able to use our total *chi* to deal with the problem at hand. But most of us can't. We must use a large portion of our *chi* simply to control ourselves, to prevent ourselves from being overwhelmed by stress. Instead of focusing and directing our energies solely to our main purpose, we give our *chi* all kinds of "minor" tasks: dealing with our panic, shock, and confusion; quieting our nerves; imposing control over our mental and physical processes.

The effect is the same as if we were trying to go through a door by pulling it open with one hand while holding it closed with a foot. Is it any wonder that we can't apply our full efforts to anything, or that we tire easily, or that we quickly become confused or distracted?

We must use part of that *chi* to deal with stress, to control ourselves. If we don't have ourselves under control, how can we ever turn to our problems? We can't, of course. At least most of us can't. But the accomplished karateist can. Because he can transcend the barrier between mind and body at will, he can direct his *chi* where and how he pleases. For the karateist, stress is not a threat that must be dealt with, but rather the fuel that fires the engine of living.

The Liabilities of Consciousness

What, exactly, is this barrier between mind and body? Is it mystical? Is it a matter of theory? Is it something all of us know well, perhaps too well? It is one of humanity's most valuable possessions: consciousness.

Consciousness is what gives us the capacity for reflection. It's what we use to solve problems. It allows us to contemplate, to meditate, to understand, to weigh and judge. It's what makes us different from the animals.

True. But I'm not suggesting that we mercilessly root it out and throw it away. I value my consciousness as much as you do yours. What I am telling you is that this marvelous faculty, this gift of evolution, is precisely what prevents us from using our full capacities. It's what divides and fragments our *chi*. It prevents our minds and bodies from working together, in total unison.

There are several reasons for this.

First, our consciousness requires—demands—that we spend some of our energy on its upkeep. It must constantly be reassured that all is well, or it starts issuing orders, some of them contradictory and senseless.

To keep our consciousness pacified, we repress, ignore, or purposely misinterpret some stimuli. We tell ourselves everything is fine when it isn't. We insist we're happy when we're sad. We pretend the situation is under control when it's really blowing up in our faces. When faced with stress, we attempt to resist it, to impose our own order and control on it, instead of letting it affect us, letting it liberate our *chi*, then using that *chi* to handle the situation.

Thus, repression reduces our ability to call forth our resources in two ways: by using up some of those resources and by preventing us from experiencing stress, the very condition that calls forth our energies.

Second, our consciousness misinforms us about our capabilities. Being neither body nor brain, it is only vaguely familiar with the abilities and limitations of each.

So, when we face a difficult situation, our consciousness often stops us in our tracks, by announcing, "Impossible." Sometimes it's right, I suppose. But far more often than we might dream, it is completely wrong.

We've all heard stories about mothers who have seen their children crushed under automobiles and, incredibly, lifted those cars single-handedly, so their children could escape. This is what total *chi* can do when it is completely focused and directed.

But suppose such a mother were to ask herself, in this situation, "Can I lift that car?" Her consciousness would provide a quick and definite answer: no! And she wouldn't be able to, even if she tried, because she wouldn't be able to focus and direct her *chi* completely.

This same thing happens to the brain. A few times in my life, I've lost an important phone number or message—something I'd hardly felt the need to glance at, since it was written down. But faced with the loss, I've attempted to remember it anyhow. If I asked myself— consciously—if I could remember the number or message, I'm sure the answer would have been, "No chance. You didn't look at it long enough." But, not letting my consciousness misinform me about my limitations, I've put my total energy to work and, astonishing all around me, remembered what was "impossible" to remember.

What I'm saying is that both the body and the brain can do far more than the conscious mind thinks they can. The conscious mind thinks it knows all about human limitations. Actually, *it imposes those limitations.*

The warnings and pessimistic predictions of the conscious mind don't necessarily prevent us from trying. After all, certain circumstances dictate an effort, no matter how unlikely success seems (when we're fighting for our lives against an enormous assailant, for instance, or doing an "impossible" amount of work). But these dire predictions do prevent us from giving our all, since they prevent us from believing—down deep—that we can succeed.

This is a clear case of our *chi* being divided and working against our apparent goals. Part of our energies go into our valiant, if half-hearted effort. But part remains to tell us that our effort is doomed. Unless the task is easier than we estimated, we wind up failing.

Third, our consciousness acts as a delaying and disrupting checkpoint between our bodies and our brains. Let me explain.

Whenever we receive a stimulus—through our sight, hearing, touch, taste, or smell—that stimulus checks in with our conscious mind, which looks it over, inspects it, and passes it along to the brain for action, if it considers action necessary. And usually when our brain conceives an action in response to this stimulus, the conscious mind must inspect that, judge it, modify it, and then okay it for transmission to the body.

There are some exceptions to this rule. For example, when we're driving, or walking, or touch-typing, or bike

riding, we bypass our conscious mind and allow both
stimulus and response to flow back and forth automatically. But this ability doesn't come easily. It takes
long, hard training to make our actions automatic. If
you don't think so, ask an accomplished tennis player
or juggler or speed reader. These people have studied
and practiced for many hours to eliminate that conscious
checkpoint that monitors most stimulus-and-response
interactions.

Let's imagine, for a moment, that it simply isn't possible to eliminate the conscious mind in such situations.

Imagine yourself in a car, driving along a fairly heavily
traveled freeway. All the things you normally see, absorb,
and respond to without a conscious thought now require
continual monitoring by your conscious mind. You must
remember to gauge your speed in relation to the other
cars. You must think about holding the steering wheel.
You must gaze at the pavement with your mind engaged.
If you had to do this, you'd be a far less efficient driver
than you are now. Your judgment wouldn't be as good,
your perception wouldn't be as far-reaching, your ability
to respond under stress would be diminished, and you'd
exhaust yourself far more quickly than usual.

Well, most of us are doing that far more often than
we think. I'm not talking now about such automatic
activities as driving, but about the normal day-to-day
challenges and demands we all face continually. We
give our conscious mind too much to do. We let it handle
tasks that don't need to be handled at all, that should
be automatic. We allow it to intervene constantly, even
when it slows us down and makes us less efficient than
we would otherwise be.

It's as though every time we wanted to go from the

living room to the bathroom, we detoured through the dining room. And we always kept the dining room fully lit and heated for just such detours. There's a time and a place for a dining room, to be sure. But there's no reason to use it every time you go from the living room to the bathroom, or to keep the lights and heat on constantly. That takes extra time and wastes energy. So does allowing our conscious mind free rein in all our activities.

Consciousness prevents us from being all we can, from putting forth total effort, from realizing our full potential.

Breath: Unifier of Mind and Body

There is no way to keep your consciousness in check, consciously, that is. Willpower won't work. In fact, willpower is a function of the conscious mind.

What will work, then?

The first people to ask this question were the ancients in China, India, and other early civilizations. They knew, as we do, that men usually were not able to perform to the limits of their capabilities. They knew that a division between mind and body existed. And they understood the enormous benefits that might come to the person who was able to unify himself.

Certain creatures in their environment did not suffer from a separation between mind and body: the animals. Confronted with a stimulus—threat, hunger, sexual desire—they responded instantly and completely.

The ancients noticed that animals' reaction times were much faster than men's. And on a pound-for-pound basis, they were also far stronger than men. They were faster swimmers or swifter runners than men. They had more endurance. They were fiercer fighters. They could be quieter, if they wished, or louder. Their sense of smell, hearing, and even sight, in some cases, was superior to man's. The ancients believed that this was because the animals were more at one with themselves. Animals' *chi* flowed undivided and unfragmented, focused exactly as intended. Their total resources were always available to them.

Long ago, men asked themselves why this was so, and if there were any way they could mobilize themselves with animal-like unity and singlemindedness. They came to the conclusion that animals possessed this unique ability because they weren't burdened with something men had: consciousness, awareness of self. This meant that in animals, nothing intervened between stimulus and response, between idea and action, between mind and body.

Certainly, animals were more limited creatures than man because they lacked consciousness. They did not have powers of deliberation, intellectualization, analysis, etc. But, in another sense, they were more than man. They were totally unified beings. They suffered from no internal confusions and conflicts.

On the face of it, there seemed no way men could take on the positive qualities of the animals. There was no way to dispense with consciousness, even if that were desirable. Nevertheless, the ancients studied the animals. They watched them under normal conditions and under conditions of stress. They watched how they reacted to emotion—to threat, to hunger, to pain.

Many animal moves intrigued the ancients. And some of these eventually became the basis for various karate postures, at least symbolically. But what fascinated them more than anything else was the way animals breathed. Their breathing pattern was different from man's. In the face of stress or threat, they inhaled sharply. Then, as they took action, they exhaled sharply. It was as if they gathered their *chi* by inhaling and released it by exhaling, or intensified their energies by drawing *in* their breath and liberated them or expended them by letting their breath *out*.

Animals faced with danger composed themselves by taking a deep breath, then lashed out as they exhaled. It was almost as if they were willfully controlling their emotions. This breathing pattern was not limited to a single species or type of animal, the ancients noted. It could be found in every kind of animal.

But not human beings. At least not all the time. Oh, it's not that we lack the instinct. There's reason to believe human beings once reacted this way as automatically as animals still do—until our conscious minds intervened.

For instance, we still gasp (inhale) in fear, at least for a moment. And we inhale when we catch a ball, or when we begin precision work that requires concentration and exactitude. And when babies cry, they tend to take a series of inward breaths, to regain control, to pacify themselves. But this occurs only in unguarded moments, when consciousness is not yet triggered (or, in the case of a baby, preconscious moments). The instant we start to think about what's happening, the pattern disappears. Under stress, we breathe in and out quickly in no particular order, without rhyme or reason. We do not use our breath to compose ourselves, to gather our *chi*, to liberate our energies in a focused or directed way.

At any rate, the ancients—especially in China and India—pondered these breathing differences between men and animals. Out of their thinking came two distinct but related breathing techniques, one a part of yoga, the other a cornerstone of karate.

In general, the karate breathing technique amounts to adopting a pattern of breathing when faced with stress. This technique allows the karateist to remain calm and composed even when his life is in danger. It allows him to focus and direct his *chi* to serve his needs, without using any of it against himself.

Used in this manner, patterned breathing serves as a vehicle and a bridge between mind and body, a way to bypass conscious thought. It allows us to react more efficiently to stimuli, to reduce the time between action and reaction, to strengthen and guide our response to stress.

Patterned breathing empties the mind of thought— or conscious thought. In this sense it works in the same way that patterned breathing does in the natural method of childbirth, where the mother-to-be is given complicated breathing patterns. As she focuses on them, during labor, her sensation of pain is greatly reduced. Meditation also aims at emptying the mind of conscious thought, substituting not breathing but the repetitious sound of a single word, known as a mantra.

Karateists see stress as the stimulator of life's energies. We believe that total freedom from stress is nothing more or less than death. And we believe that those who shield themselves from stress do so at the expense of their vitality.

What karate breathing changes is not the stress, but our reaction to it. The average person receives stress negatively. Depending on the character and intensity of the stress, he becomes anything from nervous and uncomfortable to confused and frightened. He hasn't a prayer of putting his full abilities to work.

But if that same person is able to superimpose karate breathing techniques on that stress, if he can shut off his conscious reaction to it, he will become calm and clearheaded, relaxed yet alert. He'll be able to put his full energy into dealing with the problem or event causing the stress.

The karateist works hard to link stress, not to panic or discomfort, but to calmness and steadiness. Breathing is the key. When faced with stress, the karateist automatically begins his patterned breathing. And when he begins that breathing, he automatically feels calm and in control. But that's not all that happens. The karateist's controlled breathing not only keeps him calm and composed, but also gives him a tremendous surge of energy. It liberates his *chi*, as the ancients would say.

Stress creates or stimulates the production of *chi*, you'll remember. By eliminating conscious thought, controlled breathing allows this energy, or *chi*, to flow, to become totally available to the karateist, to use as he pleases in a focused or directed manner.

Ancient Behaviorism

How does a karateist learn to associate breathing with stress? Does he walk the streets at night and, when confronted with a mugger, start puffing? Does he climb out on the ledges of high buildings, look over, and breathe? Not quite. But close.

The ancients found that the human stress response could be triggered not only by anger, fear, surprise, or sudden joy, but also by heat and cold. Sudden exposure to either extreme of temperature, they discovered, produced shock, a variety of stress. The intensity of this shock could be varied by the intensity of the temperature extreme and the length of time a person was exposed to it. They found that the body reacted to a sudden dousing with cold water in exactly the same way it reacted when threatened with actual physical harm. This gave them a way to produce a stress reaction in the body again and again, without having to search out truly threatening circumstances. So, in ancient times, karate masters practiced linking the body's reaction to stress with patterned breathing by standing under cold waterfalls.

They accomplished two things by constant repetition of this act. First, they became extremely familiar with the bodily sensations caused by stress. Second, they taught themselves to meet these sensations automatically with patterned breathing, in order to remain composed and to let their *chi* flow.

Tapping Your Energy Sources

Today we produce stress reactions with other techniques. We engage in a sort of prearranged combat. The kicks and strikes are carefully controlled, the karateists are not in any great physical danger. But they are threatened with defeat.

By repeating this situation over and over again, karateists become familiar with fear—a prime cause of stress. And they become familiar with the bodily reactions it causes. They become so well acquainted with this emotion and its effect on their bodies that it is almost a friend. This is in direct contrast to the person who avoids fear-producing situations or represses his fears, and then is powerless when the emotion actually touches him.

In fact, modern-day karateists become so familiar with fear and other strong emotions that they can create them at will, with the impact of the real thing. This is the second way we simulate stress. We imagine or fantasize fear. In this way we can create a stress reaction in our bodies at will—and without splashing ourselves with hot or cold water.

But producing this stress reaction artificially is only half of the process. The other half has to do with reacting to it, by using patterned breathing in response to it.

Each time we call forth the stress response in karate class, we instantly superimpose controlled breathing on top of it, which empties our minds of conscious thought. This, in turn, has two effects. First, it relaxes us and allows us to remain calm, steady, and composed. If we didn't use breathing techniques at this point, our conscious minds would be screaming at us to panic, to worry, to tighten up. Second, it removes the barrier that prevents the *chi* from flowing smoothly. Those conscious thoughts don't stand in the way of our response. The energy created by stress, therefore, is available to us to use in whatever way we want—but without the panic that usually accompanies it.

Actually, we're using two well-known psychological principles simultaneously. The first of these is something called desensitization. This is a way to become so familiar with something that you consider disturbing or frightening that it loses its negative impact. Psychotherapists use this technique to cure people of their phobias.

Let's say, for instance, that you're afraid of heights, yet you work in a tall building. A psychotherapist using desensitization will have you lie on a couch in his office, totally relaxed—every single muscle loose. Then he'll ask you to imagine, say, walking up a flight of stairs. He'll ask you to stop and imagine, for example, a peaceful meadow at the instant you start to feel the first signs of tension. After repeating this a number of times, you'll be able to imagine walking up that stairway without feeling tense at all. Then the therapist will repeat the procedure, having you imagine you're going up in an elevator. After that, he'll do the same, having you imagine looking out of a high window.

Finally, when you can imagine sky-diving without fear, he'll have you do the same thing while actually doing something you fear—again, starting at the lowest level and gradually working up. Eventually you'll be able to work in that skyscraper without a thought of being frightened by your distance from the ground. Your phobia will have been desensitized out of existence.

This same technique is used against fear of flying, fear of animals, even fear of sexual relations.

Karateists, by frequently creating intensely emotional (stress) situations and by experiencing them in class, similarly desensitize themselves to this feeling. It no longer calls forth panic, paralysis, nervousness, or other uncontrolled response. The karateist can remain calm and contained in the face of stress, able to use his best judgment. This is an enormous advantage in a combat situation, of course. But it's also an enormous advantage in any other stressful circumstance—such as a vital business meeting, a final exam, or an auto accident.

The second psychological principle karateists put to work is something known as a conditioned response.

I'm sure you've heard of the famous dogs Pavlov trained to salivate at nothing more than the sound of a bell. Normally, ringing bells don't make dogs' mouths water. Food does. Just as the sight or smell of food makes our own mouths water. But Pavlov—a Russian physiologist who worked from the late 1800s to the early 1900s—thought he could trigger this unconscious bodily response with something other than food.

What he did seems simple and obvious today. He rang a bell each time he fed his dogs. He kept this up for weeks. The dogs came to associate the sound of the bell with feeding time. Finally, when he felt confident that the association had been made, he sounded the bell but didn't bring the food. The dogs salivated.

Karateists used this same concept centuries before Pavlov "discovered" it. They weren't working with bells and food, of course. Instead, they were using controlled breathing and stress.

Pavlov's dogs learned to associate food with a ringing bell. Karateists learn to associate stress with controlled breathing. Take away the food—but ring the bell—and the dog salivates. Take away the stress—but breathe in a controlled manner—and the karateist's body has a stress reaction.

This point is important. Karateists can call forth a physiological stress reaction merely by altering their breathing pattern. In other words, by breathing in the proper way, karateists can stimulate their flow of energy, or *chi*, in exactly the same way it is stimulated by actual stress.

Just by breathing correctly, karateists can increase their blood pressure, heartbeat, metabolism, blood sugar, adrenalin production, etc. They can turn on all systems—in just the way a threat turns on all systems. *But without the threat.* They can mobilize all their strength and mental acuity *at will.*

The main aim of karate is to make its practitioners into complete, fully realized human beings who can call forth all their resources and use their total capabilities at will. The breathing techniques I've described are probably the most important step in achieving that goal. They permit the karateist to mobilize his complete capacity whenever he feels the need.

Imagine what this could do for you in your everyday life—how it could change your performance on the job, in sports, as you do your hobbies, in school. Imagine how it could help you in emergencies—when you're called on to do an extraordinary amount of work, or when you're given an unusually difficult task; when you're faced with an emergency that requires more physical strength or mental sharpness than you usually have; when you must confront a threat or attack; when survival might be at stake.

Supercharging: Achieving Full Potential

This breathing technique gives karateists what people often believe is superhuman strength. The karateist isn't superhuman. But he can use *all* his strength when he wants to, while most people are never able to use anything more than a fraction of their capacity.

With these breathing techniques, karateists can increase their strength up to five times its normal level. They're able to do what that mother who lifted the car off her daughter did—but without the emergency she needed to break through her consciousness barrier.

I call this ability to cause the vital energy to flow *supercharging,* because it boosts strength and brain power far above the usual, normal levels. What's more, it also supercharges the senses. In this state the karateist hears better, sees better, and is generally far more alert than usual.

Supercharging alters a karateist's level of consciousness. It lifts him above his usual perspective and gives him a sense of being in tune with the universe, in tune with all things. This special state unifies mind and body in spectacular fashion, but it is not something a karateist wants to experience constantly. It's for occasions of special need, either inside the classroom or out in the workaday world.

Once a karateist masters supercharging, he seems to change his metabolism in some permanent way, however. It's not that he's constantly supercharged. The system couldn't stand that for long. It's that he now operates at a somewhat heightened rate of sensitivity. It's as if someone has opened him up and set the "idle" higher. That's why karateists are generally more alert and more integrated people than nonkarateists, why they normally perform at a higher level even without making an effort to supercharge. It's a matter of breath intensity, of using breathing patterns appropriate to the situation.

I realize that what I'm saying isn't easy to accept if you've never experienced it. But I have experienced it— I experience it daily—and so do many of my students. I am talking about a very real, very potent phenomenon. I'm talking about a feeling you, too, can have, if you're willing to give it your time and energy.

Of course, supercharging isn't the first thing a student learns in karate class. It's more like the last thing. It's rarely taught to anyone below the black belt level. And there's a good reason for this.

If a person attempts to supercharge before he understands the limitations of his body, before he knows how much his joints and ligaments can take without snapping, how much his muscles can take without ripping, how much his circulatory system can take without popping, how much his mind can take without flipping out, he could do himself serious injury. In fact, that incident with the lady and the car that I've been talking about wound up with the lady in the hospital. She'd cracked a vertebra and strained numerous ligaments and joints.

The harm one can do to oneself by supercharging isn't limited to physical harm. Even for advanced karateists, the supercharged state can be almost hallucinogenic. In fact, some ESP experts I've talked to believe that psychics are supercharged when they perform their mental feats.

I've known some karateists who've taken supercharging too far. They've forced themselves on, higher and higher until they've very nearly lost touch with reality, increasing their physical strength and mental powers to the point of mania. For this reason, supercharging and insights into the superconscious aren't taught until a student is well advanced, until he has a clear idea of his mental and physical capacities. Even then, it's taught with care and caution. Otherwise, it would be like putting racing-car fuel into an ordinary car engine and letting it run, destroying itself.

It's only toward the end of a student's training that he is taught the *kata* that magnifies the powers of mind and body via breath control, the *sanchin*. Firm knowledge of this *kata* allows the karateist to keep a clear head regardless of the situation. This *kata* lets him liberate and focus his total *chi*.

The *sanchin*, you might say, shows man how to commit himself totally—like animals do—yet allows him to retain his humanity. Thus he transcends the division of mind and body. He becomes a fully integrated creature on a level higher than he thought possible. He gains the capacity to use his total resources and his total capacities whenever that becomes necessary. And he lives his everyday life a giant step above his former level.

Chapter 4

A Karate Appetizer

I've been talking about complicated concepts. But in this chapter I hope to make these abstract ideas more concrete by giving you at least a small sampling of the physical and mental sensations that karate creates in its practitioners.

Books and photographs are static, but karate is dynamic. The motion of the *kata* cannot be captured in still pictures, even a series of them. A movie can show you what a *kata* looks like from the outside, but it cannot capture what happens on the inside. Even if I gave you extended photographic lessons, and you copied the photographs precisely, you'd just be doing an imitation of karate. That would be worse than not doing it at all, since it might lead you to think you'd actually begun to learn the art.

Learning karate takes hard work and dedication. It also requires an instructor who will work with you personally. The relationship between student and teacher, the exchange of emotion that occurs between them, and the communication between one student and another are essential to learning karate.

What I'm about to show you can give you only the barest hint of what karate can actually be, how it can actually feel. Still, it is a taste. And I hope this taste will whet your appetite for more.

Exercises from A.D. 600

In the sixth century A.D., Bodhidharma taught his Buddhist disciples eighteen "soft" exercises. These became the basis for the earliest forms of karate. These routines taught the students how to energize themselves, how to liberate and control their *chi* and how to focus and direct it. Bodhidharma's exercises also conditioned the monks' bodies, gradually improving their health, increasing their strength, and leading them toward the spiritual development they were striving for.

Some ancient texts purporting to describe Bodhidharma's eighteen original exercises still exist, but scholars argue about their authenticity. Furthermore, these descriptions are often obviously oversimplified and sometimes even contradictory. Here's one that is still practiced today:

1. Stand with feet together, arms hanging loosely at sides.
2. Raise your arms, so that both are straight out in front of you.

3. Make your hands into fists, with your thumbs inside your fingers, squeezing tightly.
4. Pull your arms back, holding them parallel to the ground, still extended, until both are slightly behind the torso line.
5. Push your arms as far back as they can go.
6. Repeat until you tire.

If you consider this exercise simply as a series of movements, it closely resembles calisthenics. But more is happening here than simple movement.

The thumbs are tucked inside the fists—and then squeezed tight—to create pain, on a low level. The purpose: to force you to focus your consciousness (or your attention or your concentration) on your fists.

For most people, consciousness is usually centered behind the eyes. We perceive ourselves as being somehow "located" in this area. In this location, our thoughts and our focus of concentration are closely tied together. By projecting our consciousness to another part of our body, by directing our attention—in this case—toward our fists, we weaken the power our rational thoughts have over our every action. We strengthen the ability of mind and body to act as one.

In this exercise, as we spread our arms apart, pulling them back as far as they can go while still keeping our fists tight, we expand our focus of attention to include the entire area between our fists. At the same time, by straining our muscles and by causing ourselves a small amount of pain, we turn on our systems. We create a flow of adrenalin. Our pulse, our rate of respiration increases.

In a way, this exercise (and some others I will describe)

are analogous to the warmup exercises many athletes do before taking the field. Their exercises are intended to prevent muscle pulls and to keep the body limber. Karate movements such as this are intended to turn the body on, so that it can better deal with the situation at hand, whatever that situation might be.

Here's another:

1. Stand at ease, feet together, arms hanging loosely at sides.
2. Raise your arms so that both are fully extended in front of you, palms out.
3. Letting your knees flex, allow your torso to settle downward slightly, exhaling at the same time.
4. Simultaneously drop your arms and press your palms downward.

Again, this set of movements appears ridiculously simple. What makes it different from calisthenic activity is its purpose.

When you let your torso settle, you're allowing your consciousness, your weight, your attention to move to your midsection. From this position, in the center of your body, you can project it wherever you might need it.

Here's one more:

1. Assume the position you were in at the end of the previous exercise.
2. Now inhale.
3. At the same time, raise your arms straight above you, pressing your palms skyward.
4. Simultaneously straighten your torso and back.

These movements are intended to raise your consciousness upward from your midsection, eventually into your hands.

The object of all these movements, which should be repeated again and again, is to help establish mind/body unity so that the movement can proceed without the intervention of rational thought. In a sense, these exercises are the karate equivalent of repetitively practicing a tennis stroke or a golf swing. They're intended to create a pattern of movement that can be performed without having to think about it.

While these exercises have been handed down over the centuries, they are no longer the core of karate, as they were in Bodhidharma's day. Today, they are mere fragments of far more complex and lengthy movements—the *katas*.

What I've described for you here are not only fragments, but the simplest fragments I could identify. Most of the rest defy description. Even the descriptions I've provided can give you only an idea of what these simple exercise fragments look like.

What's missing, what cannot really be put into words, is the dynamics and the intensity. In actuality, the numbered steps I've described are blended. Certain movements (or parts of movements) are performed with great intensity, others in a relaxed manner. And, in the course of all of them, muscles lock and unlock.

More important than the actual movements is the concept of being able to move your center of consciousness from its normal residence behind your eyes to any other part of your body. By "consciousness," I do not mean an actual part of your mind. I'm talking about your attention, your concentration, your energy, your sensitivity, your *chi*. And when I talk about moving or focusing your consciousness, I don't mean that you actually transfer a part of your mind from one place to another. I mean that you reorient your senses so that signals to and from the chosen part take precedence over all other signals.

While many karate movements are intended to teach this ability, the fact is that all of us—whether or not we're karateists—move our consciousness from time to time. The young baby, for example, usually transfers his consciousness to his mouth, into which he puts everything in order to measure, judge, or taste it. The safecracker transfers his consciousness to his fingertips, as he twirls the dial.

Consciousness can even be transferred *outside* the body—and most of us do this daily when we drive, type, use a knife, swing a hammer, etc. In these cases the object we're using becomes an extension of our body and we concentrate our attention on it.

The ability to move consciousness from one place to another is one of the approaches to mind/body unity, to thoughtless, spontaneous action and reaction. It was this that Bodhidharma's eighteen exercises were intended to teach (in addition to their physical benefits). Exactly how he taught his exercises, no one can be certain. Their current versions—far more intricate, subtle, and extended—are taught in many different ways both in America and in the Orient. Each master seems to have his own system, and no two systems are exactly alike.

In addition to teaching students how to shift their consciousness from one spot to another, most karate systems also lay heavy emphasis on *balance* and *strength*. A mastery of these qualities allows the karateist to put his focused consciousness to work.

Balance and Strength

There's an old Chinese saying that goes, "Before you can bring your enemy to his knees, you must learn to stand up yourself." The notion of balance has long been valued among masters of the martial arts, and most have devoted a great deal of time to perfecting stances.

In karate class you'll learn various ways to center your weight so that you can remain stable in almost any standing or moving position. You'll learn how to withdraw your weight, to become incredibly light on your feet. You'll learn how to increase your apparent mass so that you seem to be two or three times heavier than you actually are.

Once you begin to understand the true nature of balance, by studying it in various standing and moving postures, you'll become capable of controlling your mass at the moment you're shifting it. This will give you what karateists call dynamic balance—the ability to move quickly and efficiently without surrendering more than a fraction of your stability.

As with the other exercises, those that teach dynamic balance are subtle and complicated. They cannot easily be put into words. But I can give you at least a glimmering of what they're like:

1. Stand approximately three feet from a wall (with the wall on your left side). Let your arms hang loose.
2. Keeping your feet a little more than shoulder distance apart, point the toe of your left foot to the side.
3. Lean as far as you can to the left, bending your left leg and allowing your right to become extended.

4. At the same moment, swing your left arm upward in an arc, making sure your palm hits the wall as your lean reaches its peak. Do not strike the wall by hardening your arm muscles, but use your arm in a whiplike fashion.

If you do this properly, you'll find that the impact with which your hand hits the wall is far greater than if you'd simply struck the wall without shifting your weight.

Karateists have a different idea of strength than most people. Usually, people think of strength in terms of how heavy a weight they can lift or how hard they can hit. They associate strength with tensed or contracted muscles. But, at least from the karate viewpoint, hard muscles have very little to do with strength. As we see it, your strength is determined by how quickly you can move your mass—your arm, say, or your leg.

When a student first comes into my school, I ask him to make his arms as strong as he can. Invariably, he holds out his arm and makes it very tense and rigid. But this doesn't make it strong. It doesn't make him capable of doing anything much with that arm. He's just holding it out in the air and getting very tired. After all, he's fighting gravity.

In karate, you'll learn that strength and power come from motion, from the speed at which you can move. Tensed muscles actually slow you down and make you weaker. Relaxed muscles allow you to move with the greatest velocity.

Try it and see for yourself. Hold your arm out in the air and make it very stiff—so that it feels strong and powerful. Then try moving it. You can't really swing very fast, can you? If you hit something, your punch wouldn't have nearly as much impact as it could have had if your arm and wrist had been relaxed and able to move more quickly.

Now loosen your arm and wave it through the air. You can get far more force into your blow than when you were holding it rigid. Part of that force comes from the increased speed, part from a whip effect.

The famous "iron palm" technique, one of the most powerful in all the martial arts, is based on this effect. Here's one way it's done:

1. Stand relaxed, feet spread to about a foot apart, arms hanging loosely at your sides. Inhale.
2. Spread your legs to about two and a half feet, allowing knees to flex slightly.
3. Go into a rapid crouch, bending your knees (though not so far as to sit on your heels) and simultaneously exhaling.
4. At the same time, bring your arm over your shoulder in a circle, imparting momentum to it by your crouching motion.
5. Allow your open palm (which should be facing toward the floor at this point) to collide with the subject of your blow.

If you do this properly, all the force you create by suddenly crouching will express itself at your palm. Your *chi* will be concentrated at this point, imparting a blow of tremendous power.

Incidentally, the same technique can be used in reverse, by starting in a crouch, arms hanging, then suddenly springing erect and allowing your arms to whip upward. In this case, the point of impact is on the top of your hands.

One of the first things you'll learn in a karate class is how motion and strength are related. You'll learn how to use your weight to increase your speed. You'll learn to shift your weight toward your target as you swing—increasing acceleration and power—and how to shift your weight just as quickly away from that target, increasing your stability.

You'll build your strength in karate, but in a very different way than you would in any other form of physical activity. You'll be conditioning your muscles, not puffing them up. You'll also be conditioning your joints, tendons, and ligaments, by stretching and toning them.

Finally, you'll come to understand that strength is increased by keeping your body soft—relaxed—until the instant you need to become hard. And when you *do* become hard, when you do tense your muscles, you'll contract only those you specifically need to accomplish your goal. You'll put all your *chi*, all your energy, in those muscles.

You'll discover, for example, that your whole arm doesn't have to be rigid or stiff to knock down an attacker or break a board in half (if you're interested in that sort of nonsense). You'll find that you can get far more power if you contract your muscles only at the moment of impact. Eventually, as you become more and more accomplished, you'll learn to concentrate your *chi* wherever you need it most—in the ball of your foot, in your fingertips, in your elbow, in your knee, even in a single knuckle.

The Katas

In some ways, karateists at practice resemble modern dancers. Working separately or together, they execute a series of motions in a fixed sequence. This sequence, this combination of stances, positions, and breathing techniques, is a *kata*.

Every martial arts system uses *katas* (or forms) as its basic method of training. The number of *katas* varies from system to system. So do *kata* styles. Chinese *katas*, for instance, emphasize circular movements. Japanese and Korean *katas* are more linear and angular.

Whatever the system, *katas* are the vehicles through which knowledge and application of karate's principles are taught. One famous karate *sensei* ("teacher") once said, "Every possible lesson that need be learned in karate is in the *katas*."

In class, students begin with the simplest *katas* and slowly—very slowly—advance to more complex ones. They start out doing the *katas* very slowly, with almost no intensity, then gradually speed them up and intensify them.

A student's performance of a *kata*—how accurately, how quickly, how completely he can do it—becomes an objective measurement of his skill. The student knows how well he's doing and so does his teacher. It's as if he were trying to master a ballet step or a piano sonata. Technical perfection comes first. After technical perfection, however, there is another step—using the *katas* in combination, or in interacting with another student, or, at the highest levels, interpreting them for oneself.

Which *katas* a student can perform and how well he can do them reveals his abilities and his limitations—at the moment. But, as with anything, those abilities can be extended through practice.

Like anything else worthwhile, of course, mastering karate involves time, energy, and dedication. That's not to say you can't get a great deal from the art if you spend only a brief time with it. You can. But why should you, since there's so much to gain by becoming really accomplished?

The goal of a dancer or a pianist is to perform a difficult work well, with great artistry. But performance itself is not the ultimate goal of the karateist. If he truly understands the art, his goal will be to internalize the lessons contained within the *katas* and to apply them to real life.

Through the *katas*, a karateist prepares himself. He develops physical and mental discipline. He becomes more physically and mentally fit. He learns balance, coordination, speed, and agility. He develops strength and endurance. He learns about his own anatomy. He comes to understand the nature of motion and change. He also learns how to concentrate more fully, how to empty his mind of conscious thought so that his body can move more spontaneously. Through the *katas*, a karateist moves toward a greater and greater unity of mind and body. He learns to energize himself and to direct his energy toward his goals, whatever they may be.

Sanchin *and Breath Control*

If a karate student truly commits himself to mastering his art, then he must learn the most important *kata* of all—the *sanchin*. This is the complete form. Within it is the essence of karate.

Nearly every martial arts system uses *sanchin*, although it may be called by another name. The *sanchin* is not only a series of moves, but also a complex breathing exercise, the best means known of developing mind/body unity and giving the karateist the ability to supercharge.

A master performs the *sanchin* deliberately and automatically. His movements are precise, accurate, and very intense. He employs many types of abdominal breathing. He both creates and burns up a tremendous amount of energy.

If you watch someone perform the *sanchin*, you'll see that at one moment it seems to flow very smoothly and beautifully, while it seems static at the next. It gives the illusion of no motion at all on one hand, and of total motion on the other. The *sanchin* thus suggests that you can be totally hard at one instant and completely soft at another. But it also suggests that nothing is totally soft or totally hard. So, *sanchin* is a physical demonstration of the *yin/yang* concept.

Literally, the word *san* means "three" and *chin* means "spirit." The object of the *sanchin* is to develop the three spirits: the body (1), the mind (2), and the unique spirit (3) that is born when the first two are united.

The third spirit is very powerful indeed. According to the ancient Chinese, it is dragonlike and immortal. That's why they also called *sanchin* the "dragon form."

Some say that the *sanchin* was the life work of Bodhidharma and, indeed, the exercise is often called Daruma (another name for Bodhidharma) breathing. Furthermore, it shows definite influences of yoga breathing techniques—which makes stronger the case for Bodhidharma's participation in its development, since he came from India.

At any rate, many scholars and practitioners of the art believe that through *sanchin*, Bodhidharma and his followers, and other great masters, achieved complete mastery of the body and full spiritual development—an enlightenment that included not only a feeling of inner peace and harmony, but also a sense of oneness with the universe.

The Feel of Karate

The simple exercises that follow won't turn you into a karateist. But they should give you a suggestion of how karate actually feels. These exercises are definitely not *katas*. They are *simplified versions* of *some parts* of karate forms. If you do them, you'll begin to understand what I mean when I say that copying gestures of karatelike moves can't teach you much about the art. What happens on the inside is the most important part of karate.

1. Turn your head to one side and push your hand against the side of your cheek, twisting your neck as far as possible. Hold your hand tight and keep pushing. Now try to turn your head back so that it's facing forward, against the pressure of your hand.

You're not going to be able to do that, I know. You shouldn't expect to. But, by trying, you'll strengthen the muscles in your neck. And you'll understand how it feels to pit a muscle against itself, how to strengthen it by exerting energy in two contradictory directions at once.

In karate, you'll use this same principle to exercise not only your muscles, but also your ligaments, joints, tendons, and interior musculature.

2. Here's a simple exercise that strengthens your internal abdominal muscles. Stand up straight but relaxed. Draw in your abdominal muscles slowly. As you are pulling in, push outward at the same time.

Take a deep breath, trying to draw the air into your lower abdomen. Your belly should puff out. Now hold the breath for a few seconds and tighten your anal sphincter. Now pull your abdomen in, compressing the air. You should feel pressure against your anal sphincter. Apply as much as you can.

In karate, what we do with the air in our lungs is as important as getting the oxygen in the first place. Breathing is not simply a matter of inhaling and exhaling. By using our breath to create pressure on our various internal muscles and organs, we exercise parts of the body we could not otherwise reach.

A karateist's strength comes partially from his being able to concentrate his energies into an isolated area of his body. Here's an exercise you can try that will give you at least a glimmering of how this feels. Although a karateist can become skilled enough to focus his *chi* in a single knuckle, that's not for a novice or a noninitiate. So we'll use a larger portion of the anatomy for practice—your arm.

Lie on your back, preferably without a pillow, but however you feel most comfortable. Now, try to relax every muscle in your body, one by one. A good way to do this is to tighten everything, then loosen everything, muscle by muscle. Take your time about this. Breathe normally. Be alert to any feelings of tension. Try not to touch any part of your body with any other part.

After you feel completely relaxed, breathe in slowly and hold it. Concentrate on your right arm. Try to make it tense—but without tensing any other area of your body. Don't make a fist, just harden every muscle in your arm until it begins to tremble. Then exhale slowly, keeping your arm stiff.

In the beginning, you'll probably feel some tension in your stomach, or in your other arm. But, with practice, you should be able to make one part of your body rigid without affecting any other part.

When you hold your breath, you are containing your *chi*. When you tense your arm, you are letting it flow into your arm—or whatever part of your body you choose. Notice that as you exhale, the tension in your arm automatically eases. You are releasing your *chi*.

Reaching Reality via Fantasy

This next exercise is the most complicated, and it's the last one I'm going to give you. It should provide at least a taste of how a karateist thinks and breathes as he's performing his art.

You may remember that when I discussed unifying mind and body, I said that karateists use their powers of fantasy (suggestion) to call forth bodily stress reactions, then respond with breathing techniques in order to direct their energy. Well, we're going to try a little of that now.

Try to recall a circumstance in which you felt extreme anxiety or fear. The more stressful the situation, the better. Pick one that really made you feel uncomfortable —maybe one that you didn't handle very well, one you're still uneasy with.

Maybe you had to give a lecture, and you were so nervous you did a poor job. Whenever you think about it, you get embarrassed. Or perhaps you had a date with an old girl friend or an old boy friend for the first time in many years, and you were very anxious about re-kindling an old spark. Perhaps you had to take a very difficult final exam, and getting into college hinged largely upon your passing the test with flying colors. You probably felt anxious, especially if you weren't prepared.

Remember, the more stressful the incident you can recall, the better this exercise will work for you. Maybe you had to walk through a bad neighborhood alone at night. Perhaps you've been attacked by a mugger or a rapist. If you've been in an automobile accident, you can try using that event. Any situation that made you feel very anxious or fearful will do.

Once you select the circumstance you're going to recall, sit back, close your eyes, and think back to the time of the incident. Don't just visualize the specific incident itself, but imagine what happened before the incident.

Remember what you were doing that morning, the clothes you were wearing that day, the place where you were. Put yourself into the picture. Make your daydream as vivid as possible. Surround yourself with as many of the actual sights, sounds, colors, people, and conditions as you can remember. Construct a movie in your mind, with yourself as the principal player.

As you start to think about the incident, you'll probably begin to feel more and more tense. You'll get butterflies in your stomach, or you'll feel lightheaded. Your fingers may turn cold. You may start to sweat. The more realistically you've re-created your situation, the more intense your feelings will be.

If you don't feel much, don't worry about it. You may have picked the wrong incident, or you may be too distracted to concentrate. Find a quiet spot, pick a time when you won't be bothered, and try again. Eventually you'll feel more and more anxiety or nervousness.

Now stop imagining—but don't destroy your mood. Instead of thinking of the past, try to notice how you're feeling, physically. How is your body reacting to your tension?

Everybody experiences these emotions a little differently. I know some people who feel tension primarily in their jaws, others who get headaches. Some people feel nauseated, while others tremble all over. Some people get clammy hands, others get goose bumps.

But there is one physiological reaction to stress that everyone experiences. You'll notice it in yourself. It's the way you breathe. When you're feeling anxious or afraid, you take short, quick, shallow breaths. If your emotion is very tense, you may even hold your breath from time to time.

By doing this, you're trying to fight down the unpleasant emotions you feel. Your anxiety or fear is so uncomfortable for you—physically as well as emotionally—that your first response is to push it away. Your body tries to block your breathing in an effort to block the emotion, to keep it from expressing itself. You're trying to hide how you're feeling—from yourself.

We all know what happens when we repress our reaction to stress over a long enough time—mental or physical disturbances, or both. But karate offers a way to overcome this suppression, to let your emotions flow freely, and to mobilize your *chi* to handle your problems.

Now go back to that fantasy. Start at the beginning and visualize the incident as you did before. You'll be able to tell from your breathing just how anxious you're making yourself feel.

When you find that you're breathing quickly and shallowly, force yourself to breathe deeply and slowly. Draw the air into the lower part of your abdomen, counting slowly to three. Then exhale, also to a count of three. Continue doing this for awhile—ten or twenty breaths. Don't take in so much air that you feel uncomfortable, or exhale so forcefully that you feel a strain. Try to keep your breathing regular and slow.

After a few moments, you'll find your anxiety is slipping away. No matter how hard you concentrate on your stressful situation, you'll be unable to remain tense. If your fingers were cold, they'll warm up. If you were sweating, you'll stop. If you had a headache, it will begin to fade. Your stomach will settle down.

Don't stop your fantasy. Continue to daydream, as you breathe deeply. Your breathing will release whatever tension your fantasy creates, instantly. The harmful effects of stress won't build up. You won't feel the need to repress your emotions.

Eventually, with repeated practice, you'll be able to avoid a tension buildup during actual stressful events. You'll learn to recognize the mildest signs of anxiety within yourself, and you'll be able to deal with them long before they get out of hand.

Through karate, you'll be much less likely to suffer from the accumulation of stress, or from the suppression of emotions with which you feel uncomfortable. Believe it or not, it takes a great deal of energy to repress or deny those feelings. When you stop using your energy this way, you'll find you have more than enough energy available to you for all your other activities.

It's important to keep in mind that when you're releasing tension through deep breathing techniques, you're not eliminating stress. You're just lessening its harmful effects and freeing your energy toward more productive goals.

Since stress triggers our *chi*, you can see why it's necessary for a karateist to be able to create at will a stress response in his own body. That is what you did during the last exercise.

Besides using his ability to fantasize, a karateist can also create a stress reaction by breathing rapidly and shallowly. He can alternate his breathing pattern to create or burn off as much energy as necessary.

Another way the karate student can create stress is to engage in combative maneuvers during karate class. This is how he learns to use and deal with the most extreme stress reaction of all—his fear.

Of course, learning to create stress at will and to deal with it effectively takes time. Eventually a karate student can learn to create the subtlest sort of a stress reaction. But this takes a lot of training.

Unfortunately, some students are never able to develop their imaginations enough to simulate stress conditions successfully. They must rely on real stress situations to develop their karate skills. Other people get discouraged because developing an imagination that's strong enough may take a long time.

Someday soon I plan to begin using bio-feedback techniques and equipment in karate classes. I think this will shorten the time it takes to prepare a student to learn to deal with stress. And it will be an excellent device for people who are unable to fantasize well enough to create a very strong stress response. With bio-feedback equipment, a student will be able to detect the beginnings of his stress response, and he will learn to amplify and magnify his response so that he can work with it.

Not every student who has trouble in karate is unable to create artificial stress. Some students are continually under too much stress, and no matter what they do they can't deal with it. They're constantly anxious or fearful and are really unable to perform because they can't manage to harness their energy, to control it in any useful way.

Bio-feedback will help this type of student too. He'll be able to seize on those moments of lesser anxiety and learn to make himself more calm. When he can deal with some of his increased energy, he'll be better able to work with it and to direct it into some productive goal.

Some students find they simply can't cope with the increasing amounts of stress they must deal with in order to progress in karate. Of course, this isn't supposed to happen. Karate instructional systems are designed to prepare students to handle each increasingly difficult level of training.

But no system, not even in karate, works for 100 percent of the people 100 percent of the time. Some students quit before they become accomplished enough to feel and appreciate the larger benefits of the art. A good teacher won't just let a student walk away, however. He'll encourage the student to stay and build his confidence.

Chapter 5

Fine-tuning Your Body

However you look at it, one of the most important things in life—if not *the* most important—is having a sound body. We all want to be physically fit and healthy. Few of us are, at least to the extent we should be.

Karate can make you physically fit, if you commit yourself to it. In fact, there is no single physical self-improvement program that can match it. Karate is also a path to better health. It helps improve some conditions and makes you more resistant to others.

From everything I've been able to discover, I can tell you that karate may also be the best method of weight control yet invented. And it is one of the few physical activities open to those with handicaps. From what I've seen in my classes, the worse your physical condition—

barring serious organic disease—the more you need karate and the more it will help you.

I know you may be tempted to take some of these statements with a grain of salt. But I intend to show you exactly why they're true, in detail.

Components of Physical Fitness

If you're like most people, you hear the words "physical fitness" and cringe. You conjure up images of recruits dressed in shorts and T-shirts doing jumping jacks on an athletic field. Nothing very appealing about that. I'll be the first to admit it. I've done some jumping jacks in my day. Boring.

Before the twentieth century, physical fitness was something Americans never had to be concerned about. Our lives required a great deal of physical exertion, and we had what it took to live. We didn't have any choice. We plowed our fields and built our houses and hunted our food. We scrubbed our laundry and hauled our packages and beat our rugs.

Then came the automobile, the vacuum cleaner, the washing machine, the tractor. Technology and America took to each other. Society adapted to the machine age. Maybe we adapted too well for our own good.

It wasn't until long after we'd become quite entrenched in our sedentary way that its dangers became apparent: heart disease, obesity, more rapid aging, arthritic diseases, hardening of the arteries, and so on. The medical profession began promoting the value of exercise. Then the government began pushing physical fitness. And the schools started to upgrade their physical education programs. Slowly, Americans began to get concerned. Evidence supporting the benefits of exercise mounted.

Today, everyone believes in physical fitness. It's become American again. Everybody knows he should have it. Some people are even trying to get it. But hardly anybody really knows what it is. Even those who want it most may be going after it the wrong way.

Physical fitness refers to development and maintenance of the body in six specific areas: strength, endurance, speed, flexibility, balance, and coordination. For basic, all-around fitness, everyone—no matter how inactive—should be in good shape in all these areas.

Most Americans, even those trying to sweat and groan their way to fitness through various exercise programs and sports, are tragically far from genuine, basic, all-around fitness. Usually, one or more areas have been totally ignored. Take a closer look at the aspects of physical fitness and you'll see what I mean.

1. *Strength* is what you need to take your groceries from the car to the kitchen, open a stuck window, jump across a puddle, pull a stubborn weed from your garden, lug a bulging briefcase to and from the office. We acquire strength by conditioning our muscles, through exercise. You'll want firm, well-toned muscles throughout your entire body, not just in your arms, but in your legs and stomach as well.

So any good fitness program will exercise all the muscle regions. But it won't—it shouldn't—make you into a muscleman (or woman). Let's face it. Large, overdeveloped muscles aren't attractive. And they usually don't work very efficiently, either.

2. *Endurance,* or stamina, is what you need to perform

any activity over a long period of time. You need endurance to spend a full day on the job, even if you're sitting at a desk. You need it to stand on line at the movies, to mow your lawn, to shop, to go from your basement workshop to your bedroom on the second floor and back. You can increase your endurance by strengthening your heart and exercising your lungs. An adequate fitness program must include some activity strenuous enough to raise your heart rate and make you breathe more oxygen into your lungs.

3. *Speed* refers to reaction time and to how quickly you can move any part of your body, or any combination of parts, or your whole body. You need speed to catch a dish that slips out of your hand, to keep up with an active toddler, to run after your commuter train, to avoid a rear-end collision when the car in front of you stops suddenly. A fitness program should help you build speed by requiring you to increase the number of times you can properly perform complex movements within a certain time period.

4. *Flexibility*, or suppleness, enables you to stretch for a book on the top shelf, bend down to tie a shoe, fold up to climb into a compact car, twist around to see what's behind you. Even if you're not very limber to begin with, you can increase your suppleness by practicing bending and stretching.

5. *Balance*, or a sense of equilibrium, is what keeps you on your feet. It prevents you from falling if you trip over a loose piece of carpet while you're going up the stairs. It allows you to remain steady while you're on a tall ladder rescuing your cat from a tree. It keeps you out of another passenger's lap if the plane you're on hits an air pocket while you're in the aisle. A physical

fitness routine will help you develop a better sense of equilibrium by requiring you to maintain a precarious position for a brief period of time.

6. *Coordination,* or skill, is what you need to perform any set of complex actions with precision, grace, and efficiency. Without coordination you can't button your coat or write your name. You can't ride a bike. When you're not very well coordinated, you look clumsy and feel uncomfortable. Coordination is a product of balance, flexibility, speed, and strength.

But what does fitness mean in real life? How can you tell if you're physically fit?

Fitness isn't the same for everyone. It's relative. For one thing, fitness depends on your age. If you're twenty-five years old, physical fitness isn't the same for you as it is if you're sixty. Physical fitness also depends on your sex. Fitness doesn't mean the same thing for women as it does for men.

Another thing fitness depends on is your general health. If you've never been sick, then fitness is different for you than if you've just had surgery, or if you have an organic illness, or if you're handicapped in some way.

Another thing fitness is relative to is how you're built. Fitness for a tall person isn't exactly the same as fitness for someone shorter. If you have a slender frame, then fitness isn't the same for you as it is for someone with more bulk.

Remember, we're talking about what it means to be physically fit in real life. That's what karate is all about —dealing with life. For most people, life is unrelated to deep knee bends.

Physical fitness means being capable of doing all the things your normal, everyday life requires of you plus

a little extra—without exhausting yourself. In other
words, fitness is relative to need. Physical fitness means
that you have enough strength, enough endurance,
enough flexibility, enough speed, enough balance, and
enough coordination to see you through an average
day, with some reserve capability to bring you through
minor emergencies.

Let's start with daily needs. What determines them?
First of all, your job—what you do all day long. If you're
a lineman for the telephone company, fitness means one
thing. If you're a bookkeeper, it means another. And
still another if you make your living selling real estate,
and yet another if you sell umbrellas in a department
store. If you're a housewife with a toddler, fitness isn't
the same for you as it would be if you had three grown
children.

How you get to and from your job is almost as important as the work itself when you're considering your
fitness needs. If you ride a commuter train or bus, your
needs are different than if you walk a mile to the office
each day, or drive, or take the subway.

Your daily needs don't merely consist of how you get
to your job and what you do once you're there. They
also include what you do in your leisure time. So when
you're thinking of fitness, you have to think of your life
style and your special likes and dislikes as well.

If you enjoy participating in weekend sports, then
fitness isn't the same for you as fitness for someone with
a more relaxed life style. If you like to see a movie or
play bridge on weekday evenings, then fitness doesn't
mean the same thing for you as it does for the person
who only goes out on Saturday nights. If you spend those
Saturday nights dancing in a discotheque, then fitness

isn't the same for you as it is for a person who prefers the theater. What kind of a place do you go home to after the band packs up or the curtain falls? If you live in a fifth-floor walkup, your needs are different than if you live in a ranch house.

Keep in mind that your daily routine isn't supposed to exhaust you. If you're dragging through most of your days and drained by bedtime—and you're not sick—then you're in poor shape. This isn't fitness.

Remember, fitness also includes a reservoir of strength, stamina, and all those other components I described. Since life hardly ever goes according to a master plan, you never can tell when you're going to have to put out a little extra. You should be able to do it safely, without dangerous strain.

What kind of unexpected situation should you be prepared to handle? That depends to some extent on how active you normally are. A minor emergency for a dock worker could be a major crisis for a magazine editor who's no more physically active off the job than on. You don't have to be a superman to be fit, but you've got to be able to stretch without hurting yourself.

By this time, you've probably figured out whether you're fit according to your needs. If you're like most Americans, my guess is that you can make it through the day without feeling worn out, but with little to spare. Unless you develop a reserve, you're not fit.

Fitness isn't only relative to need, however. It's also relative to what you want. If you can survive an hour-long stretch of hard tennis, but you'd like to be able to go on for two hours, then you may be as fit as you need to be, but you're not as fit as you want to be. If you've been driving to the station every day, but you'd like to be able to ride your bike instead, perhaps you're as fit as you need to be, but not as fit as you'd like to be.

Of course, everybody wants something different. But most people want—at the minimum—to be fit for their needs. I can guarantee you that karate, if you stick to it, will develop the reserve that is the difference between being fit and unfit. And if your other fitness wants aren't way out of line with your age and general health, karate can probably help you there too—if you make the commitment.

Karate can help you realize physical fitness to the maximum extent possible, given your sex, build, general health, and age. But even more important, karate can help you maintain that fitness against the ravages of time. How often have you said to yourself, "I'm just not as young as I used to be"? If you haven't felt that way from time to time, then you certainly know people who have. This realization usually strikes you when you're trying to do something that once was very easy, and you discover, to your surprise, that it's become very difficult.

You already know that your body declines with age, and so do your physical abilities. That's a fact. You probably don't like to think about it too much. None of us does, so we forget that it's not enough simply to *become* physically fit. We also have to *maintain* our fitness by *increasing* our level of activity.

Keeping active, exercising your body, helps counteract the effects of time. That's also a fact—one too many people ignore. If you don't do anything to keep yourself fit, then your condition will deteriorate very rapidly. You will no longer be fit for your needs. Much sooner than you want to, you'll have to change your life style so that it requires less of you. You'll be forcing yourself to look, feel, and act old long before it's time.

There's no way you can stop the aging process, but you can slow it down. Through karate, you can live more actively, more vitally, more productively, and more youthfully for more years.

Your Way to Fitness

You can choose from any number of activities that will make you more fit than you already are. But you can't choose a better one than karate.

Why? Because more than any other activity I can think of—and I've tried a great many of them—karate can make you truly fit. To be fit all over, you've got to give every single part of your body some work to do. So you need an activity that requires you to use everything you've got. All your parts.

That's what exercise means: using all your parts. Only by moving everything can you get total exercise. Karate is the total exercise. Its forms—the *katas*—touch you all over, and they touch you deeply. That means they affect your insides as well as your outside. They make use of your internal muscles as well as your external ones. The *katas* don't just get the outside of your body into shape. They exercise the muscles inside your abdomen and back, which support your internal organs.

Maybe you didn't even know that the muscles deep within you could be exercised. These muscles are very difficult to exercise. It's almost impossible to move most of them voluntarily—unless somebody teaches you how.

These muscles, which are made up mostly of smooth muscle tissue, can be exercised only by breathing in certain ways.

It is worth repeating: proper breathing is crucial in karate. You can't do a *kata* accurately if you don't breathe the way you should. It's as much a part of the form as how you move your arms and legs. If you're only going through the external motions, you're not practicing karate. Only someone who doesn't know much about it will think you're a karateist.

Through the *katas*, we learn to increase or decrease our respiration rate, control the amount of air we inhale and the manner in which we exhale. These various breathing patterns create internal pressure against our various organs and cause our internal musculature to move, to be exercised. You should have gotten some idea of what this pressure feels like when you tried out the techniques I described earlier.

There's no other activity that develops your body more completely than karate. That's because the *katas* make you move your body in every direction it can possibly go. This means you've got to move—to exercise—everything. You've got to use every single muscle group in each and every part of your body, inside and out.

Take your arm, for example. The karate forms don't just exercise the muscles in your upper arm, or the muscles in your forearm. They don't just require use of your wrist, or your shoulders, or the back of your arm, or the front. When you do a *kata*, you're exercising the whole arm. When you get finished, there won't be anything an arm can do that your arm hasn't done. If you keep up your karate, your arms will be fit, your legs will be fit, your entire body will be fit—it will be able to do what you ask it to, and more.

Why Pick Karate?

I've been telling you that karate is by far the best physical fitness program you can find. But you may think there's something else that will serve you just as well. All right then, let's do some comparisons.

Tennis. As a game and a sport, tennis is deservedly popular. It also has obvious physical fitness benefits. If you play frequently enough and hard enough, you'll increase both your stamina and your coordination.

But, just as obviously, tennis is not a total exercise. It does a lot for certain arm and leg muscles, but leaves other muscles, along with many torso muscles, unexercised. Besides, to play tennis, you need a partner, a court, and equipment. You can do karate at home, alone, without any special equipment or clothing.

If you're a tennis player, by the way, you may want to take up karate not only for its physical fitness benefits, but also for its ability to improve your hand-to-eye coordination. Karate can make you a better tennis player. In fact, karate can improve your performance in almost any sport.

Jogging will give you good springy muscle tissue in your legs—just the kind you want. But you'll have to find some other way to develop and exercise the rest of your body.

Many people feel that jogging is not only good for their bodies, but good for their minds as well, since it is mentally undemanding. But tension experts are now saying that in order to become truly diverted, you need something else to concentrate on. Karate, because it requires something from your mind, is a genuine diversion.

Bicycling. Once you get yourself into shape, you can really enjoy bicycling. And it will help you stay in shape, by giving your circulatory system a good workout. Like jogging, bicycling is also excellent for leg development. But, also, like jogging, it doesn't do much for your other muscles.

Karate exercises and develops all your muscles. Among other things, it builds strength and endurance. So, if you're an inveterate bicycle rider, karate can make this activity even more enjoyable for you.

Swimming is good for your legs, terrific for your arms, and excellent for your heart and lungs. If there were no such thing as karate, I'd say that swimming was the best physical fitness activity around.

But swimming, good as it is, isn't total exercise, since it does nothing for the internal musculature or organs. And, of course, it requires a pool. If you're fond of swimming, stick with it—but take up karate, too. You'll soon find you can swim faster and for longer distances.

Weight lifting will make your muscles huge, but it won't necessarily make them strong. You get strength from well-conditioned muscles; size doesn't count. Moreover, large muscles give you extra pounds to tote around. Unless your heart can cope with the added weight, you're in danger—as much danger as you'd be in if it were pure fat. Speaking of fat, that's what those muscles you get from lifting weights will turn to if you don't maintain them.

Isometrics are supposed to get you into shape in a minute and a half a day, without any other exercise. Sound too good to be true? It is.

When you do an isometric exercise, you tense one muscle against another. Or you contract your muscle against something else, like a wall or a piece of furniture. The muscle, meeting total resistance, doesn't move (hence the name isometric—still or static).

You're supposed to hold this position for about six seconds—with nearly (but not all) of your strength. But if you push too hard, you can hurt joints, ligaments, and tendons—or tear a muscle. Also, isometrics doesn't allow blood to flow freely into muscle tissue, so it doesn't develop much. And it can be performed with only a few muscle groups.

I'm not saying that isometrics has no place in a fitness program—it does. But you've got to understand the principle—and know your own body—before you can use it properly. Even then, you can't rely *entirely* on isometrics for fitness.

Calisthenics are a type of isotonic exercise. In isotonics, you pit opposing muscles against each other, but both muscles are moving. Each provides the other with some resistance. This allows for motion and exercise. The idea of a contracted muscle in motion is also expressed in the phrase "dynamic tension," the old Charles Atlas label for isotonics.

Useful as they are, isotonic movements cannot exercise your body as completely or efficiently as can one performance of a karate *kata*.

Team sports (soccer, basketball, volleyball, football, etc.). Rare is the American who hasn't dabbled in one or more of these at one time or another. They provide active pleasurable hobbies for many.

But no team sport equals karate when it comes to physical fitness benefits. None of them exercises your *entire* muscular system, or your internal musculature. Besides, you shouldn't rely on a team sport for physical fitness, since it requires so much space and so many other people. You probably won't do it regularly enough to get all the physical fitness benefits it can provide.

If you enjoy team sports, you will benefit from karate. It will give you the energy, the strength, the agility, the coordination you need to play your chosen sport at your maximum capability.

I want to emphasize here that I am not putting down any one of these activities—with the possible exception of weight lifting. They're all, in their various ways, valuable, pleasurable, or both. I'm just trying to show you that for building physical fitness, there's nothing that equals karate.

How is it that karate makes you physically fit while more traditional Western activities fail? Karate exercises more muscles and muscle groups than any other type of exercise you can do, and benefits your internal systems as well—your organs, ligaments, joints, nerves, and blood vessels. You got some idea of how this happened when you tried out the karatelike techniques and breathing routines I described earlier.

A karate-developed body is substantial, both inside and out. This all-over fitness is achieved through the *katas*. I've already told you what the *katas* are, but I want to stress again what a complete exercise they provide. It's really difficult for anyone to appreciate the truth in what I'm saying, unless they learn a *kata* or two. And if I'm doing what I hope to be doing with this book, you'll be finding that out for yourself.

But let's get back to specifics. Let's see how karate develops you in each of the six physical fitness areas I described earlier. And let's see what this development can mean for you.

Strength, Endurance, Speed, Coordination, Balance, Flexibility

Strength. You may have by now changed your original idea of what strength is. You know that karate can make you many times more powerful than you already are. The secret is in the concept of soft and hard. First of all, a combination of soft and hard techniques conditions and tones the muscles far more effectively than hard exercise alone. So in karate, you build better muscles—the raw material of strength.

But well-conditioned muscles aren't the only factor in strength. Knowing what to do with those muscles is also part of what makes you strong. In karate, you learn that your strength will be more effective if you combine the hard and soft than it will be if you simply come on hard, with all the force you can muster.

In other words, as a karateist, you would not force open a stuck door and find yourself rushing headlong into the house at breakneck speed, carried unwillingly along by your own momentum. You'd just open the door, period.

By combining the hard and the soft approaches, you would: (a) direct your strength (by using only the muscles needed to achieve a task), and (b) control your strength (by timing your actions to end with the application of strength).

Endurance. You'll remember I said earlier that the way to increase your stamina is by exercising your heart and lungs. Since breathing is such an integral part of karate, it's pretty obvious that while you're doing the *katas*, you're also giving your lungs a good workout. But you're doing more than that. You're also learning breath control. Learn the *katas* and you learn when to fill your lungs with air, how much air to fill them with, how fast to take the air in, how long to hold it, and how fast to let out how much of it. That about says it all. There's nothing else that does all this for you and your lungs.

How does karate help your heart? Well, the activity of the *katas* makes your heart beat faster. That means your *heart* is getting exercise. When you regularly increase your heart rate through activity, you end up with a lower resting pulse rate—evidence that the exercise is actually making your heart stronger and capable of bearing a greater load.

In karate, you steadily increase your endurance by steadily increasing the intensity with which you perform the *katas*.

Speed means more than just being able to move out quickly. It also means being able to move any single part of your body fast. It means fast reflexes and quick reaction time.

Karate develops speed in all these ways. At first, you learn to do the *katas* slowly, but after a short while, you'll pick up speed. You'll be amazed how fast you can actually move. You'll find that your reflexes have increased and your reaction time decreased—without your seeming to make any special effort toward that end.

By the time you can do a *kata* quickly, you will have achieved a degree of mind/body unity. You won't need to think consciously of what you want your body to do. And when you're not thinking, you can move more quickly. You don't slow yourself down. You maintain your speed until you don't need it anymore, until the very end of your movement. In other words, a karateist doesn't ride his brakes. He only puts them on when he wants to stop.

Let me give you an example. Suppose I showed you a box marked *150 lbs.* and asked you to pick it up. Your first reaction would probably be, "Oh, I can't do that." But let's say I convinced you to try.

You'd bend down and put your hands on the box, thinking something like this: "That's a heavy box. No one is going to help me pick it up. Even if I manage it, I won't be able to go very far with it. And I'll probably hurt my hands and strain my arms. Besides, I'm probably not strong enough to pick it up."

If you then tried to pick up the box, you'd be unlikely to give it your best effort. You'd make a show, of course—even to yourself. But you'd hold back, at least a little. Do you see how your thoughts can make you ride the brakes?

Now imagine what would happen if I showed you the same box—only this time with a *75 lbs.* sign on it. You wouldn't be worried about hurting yourself. You'd have no reason to put the brakes on too soon. You'd lift the box—perhaps with a bit of a struggle—but you'd lift it, since you know you can raise 75 lbs.

My point here: karate will teach you how to use your capacities to their fullest, when you have to. You'll become capable of pulling out all the stops.

Coordination is skill in moving your body. The more complex the movement, the more coordination you need. One of the most important benefits of karate is that it will improve your coordination. It will make you more graceful and less clumsy. You become more coordinated by performing the *katas*, which involve breathing and moving at the same time, sometimes in patterns that are quite complex. In fact, karate teaches you to perform very complex motions automatically.

Balance is what gives you the ability to be mobile. As you walk or run, you are first in balance, then you step out and off-balance yourself, then you recapture your balance once again. To the degree that you can control this balance/off-balance process, you will be able to move confidently and with agility.

How can karate help you here? By teaching you the art of dynamic balance. Dynamic balance is what enables you to maintain stability even while you're in motion.

When you perform a *kata*, you're in constant motion. You learn how to shift your weight from one position to another. You learn how to feel comfortable when both feet aren't on the ground. You learn how to move. And you learn how to remain steady—even under adverse circumstances.

Flexibility. If you have a supple body, you can move it easily in all directions. You can bend and twist and stretch, without straining your muscles or pulling on your joints.

You develop suppleness by moving. The object of the *katas* is to move every part of your body as far as it can possibly go in every conceivable direction. Karate will make your body more elastic, more resilient, and more capable of moving any way you want it to.

Fitness Through Karate

What can fitness do for you besides making you function better—by giving you the strength, stamina, flexibility, etc., you need to live your daily life? Well, it can also make you *feel* better. And that opens up new possibilities for satisfying activity.

When you're fit, you feel more energetic. You want to do more, you want to experience more, you want to try new things—and because you've been developing your body through karate, you're able to do many things you never thought possible before.

Karate will teach you to use all your faculties to the maximum. Even your vision, hearing, and other senses will become sharper through karate training. It's all a part of developing your awareness. It's a way of turning yourself on to a whole new life. That's what karate does—teaches you to turn on all your systems and keep them operating as close to their youthful peak as possible. If you begin karate when you're young, you will prolong your youth. If you start when you're older, you will recapture much of the youthful vitality you've lost.

How fast are you going to notice the effects of karate? As soon as you begin karate, you will start to improve your fitness level. But that doesn't mean you'll *notice* the change immediately.

If you're in pretty good shape to begin with, then a small improvement in your fitness level won't make much of a change in how you function and feel. So the initial effect of karate will be more subtle than it will be for someone who's in really bad condition. If you're run down and out of shape, then that initial improvement is going to make you feel very different. You'll notice within a few weeks that your body is becoming more capable and more fit. And you'll also start feeling more energetic. Karate really works fastest for those who need it the most.

Many people think that physical fitness means better health. Actually, fitness gives you a generally healthy feeling, contributes to your sense of physical well-being, and probably extends your life, but it doesn't guarantee immunity from organic disease. But because karate makes you physically fit inside and out, and because it also gives you a safe way to handle stress, karate—more than any other activity I know of—can raise your resistance to many diseases. Sometimes health problems even disappear after taking up karate.

Many students have told me how their health has improved since they began karate. The health improvements they mention fall mainly into four different areas:

1. stress-related diseases such as ulcers and hypertension
2. back problems, especially lower back difficulties and disc problems
3. respiratory diseases such as asthma
4. psychosomatic illnesses.

Actually these categories overlap, because stress can cause or contribute to asthma, back pain, or psychosomatic ailments. Once you learn how to use stress safely as a trigger for your *chi*, you naturally lower the possibility of becoming ill from it.

I want to tell you about some experiences of my students, who feel karate has made them healthier.

A case in point is George Y. George is fifty-one years old and a highly competitive businessman who battles his way through New York City's garment center every day. George started taking karate because his son in California took it up and told George he ought to try it. George had been coming to class for three months before he came into my office to tell me his story.

George said, "I think you've got a cure for high blood pressure here."

"Go on," I said. I'd heard this from other people before, but I didn't want to spoil the story for George.

"My doctor's been worried about my climbing blood pressure for five years. Last year he told me that if my pressure kept going up the way it has been, I had maybe another two or three years before I'd have to start medication."

"I can already guess what's happened," I told George. "You went to the doctor and your blood pressure's down."

"Yep. For the first time in six years. We were both really surprised, let me tell you."

"How can you be sure it's karate?" I asked. "Could be any one of a hundred different things that's caused the change."

"No. I sat with the doctor for forty-five minutes yesterday and together we figured out that the only thing that's different about my life now is the karate. I eat the same, sleep the same, work even harder and worry even more. No, it's the karate all right."

Another of my students, Al W., is a thirty-two-year-old photographer who has suffered from asthma ever since he was a child. When Al first came to the school a year ago, he told me about his asthma and asked me if I thought he could have an attack during karate class. He was a little concerned because he'd tried to get involved in other activities from time to time and sometimes they'd triggered a serious bout of wheezing.

I told Al that I couldn't promise anything, but I felt that he wasn't likely to have any difficulty with karate, since learning how to breathe properly is such a vital part of the skill. I also told him I'd seen karate have a beneficial effect on several asthmatic children, and I saw no reason why it might not benefit him as well.

Turns out that karate has helped Al tremendously. He hasn't experienced a single attack since he began. "In fact, I'm convinced I'm cured," he told me.

It seems that karate has truly worked wonders for Al W. And I've seen other asthmatics who've improved after taking up karate.

But, if you are *not* in generally good health, please check with your doctor before beginning karate. And if he gives you the go-ahead, do not expect it to be a cure-all. Karate might help you, but the important thing is that you enjoy it without hurting yourself.

At the very least, karate will make you more physically fit. But there's also the possibility that you'll get other health benefits from it as well.

Bypassing Handicaps

Karate is one of the few physical activities that is open to handicapped people. You should keep in mind that karate is designed not only to minimize your liabilities, but also to turn those liabilities into assets.

The karate *katas* are very versatile. They can be modified to suit your particular needs. There are an infinite variety of moves in karate. Your teacher can emphasize those that lend themselves best to your special abilities.

He'll be doing that anyway, whether you're handicapped or not. In a sense, everyone is handicapped to some degree, because everyone has weak points as well as strong. If you are handicapped, you have nearly as many assets as a nonhandicapped person. The main difference is that your weaknesses are more visible.

A nonhandicapped person can hide his weaknesses. He may not even be aware of them. But once he begins karate, he has to deal with them. He's got to ferret them out and work on them, the same way a handicapped person must. Neither of you may be able to change your weaknesses, but you can both learn to compensate.

So if you have a handicap, don't rule out karate. You may well be able to become very proficient and to enjoy it.

Weight Control for Life

There's hardly a person in America who isn't worried about being overweight—or doesn't know someone who is. If you're not overweight, then your spouse is, or your mother, or your best friend, or somebody else fairly close to you. If you don't know anyone who thinks he's too fat now, then you surely know someone who worries about becoming too fat in the future.

Diet clubs abound all over the country. The diet-food industry comes out with something new every month or so. Even diet doctors and diet pills are popular, though it's common knowledge that diet pills are very dangerous. Fad diets keep appearing, new ones every year. And people keep trying them, even though they know they're useless or dangerous or both.

Hardly any diets work, though. Very few of the people in America who lose weight manage to keep it off over a period of five years. Only 2 percent keep it off for ten years. If you're one of those people who've tried and failed—over and over and over—take heart. There's hardly anyone I know who has committed himself to karate who hasn't been able to shed excess pounds and *keep them off.*

Hardly a day goes by that I don't hear a comment from one student or another about how karate has helped them reach a desired weight and keep those pounds off. Comments like these:

> "I never get as hungry as I used to. Before I started taking karate, I was snacking between each meal. Now I'm completely satisfied with three meals a day. I don't even crave snacks" (a piano teacher).
>
> "I eat exactly what I used to eat, but I've lost weight and I don't seem to be gaining it back. Must be because I've gotten more active" (an industrial engineer).
>
> "I was up and down on the scales. I'd diet off five or six pounds, then eat like there was no tomorrow and put it back on—plus more. I've tried every diet in the books, and some that were never written down anywhere. I started taking karate a year ago, lost ten pounds in two months and haven't put an ounce of it back on. I think it's because karate has taught me discipline. And it feels good" (a research assistant).

I could fill pages with testimonials like these. But I'd rather tell you why karate is so good for weight control. There are several reasons:

1. You exercise. Everyone knows that the more active you are, the more calories you burn up. Going to a

karate class keeps you intensely active for an hour or more. Furthermore, you get a good workout when you practice at home. And when it comes to losing weight, the more exercise you get, the faster you'll lose.

2. Your metabolism changes. Since karate turns all your systems on, you start running at a fast idle instead of a slow crawl. You burn up more fuel. Several students have told me their doctors found a measurable change in their metabolism rate after they started taking karate.

3. Your way of moving changes. After you've been studying karate for a little while, you'll begin to notice that you move your entire body with more speed and energy as you go about your daily tasks. You walk more briskly, get out of chairs more quickly, bound up and down stairs. You don't drag yourself around so much. These may seem like very small changes, but they all add up to using those calories.

4. Karate moves blood away from your stomach and to other parts of your body. This means you experience less hunger. Some karate students, if they feel a desire to eat the wrong food at the wrong time, simply do a *kata* or two. Then they're not hungry anymore.

5. Karate makes you more relaxed and decreases free-floating anxiety and undirected nervousness—often the cause of overeating. You don't need food—or any other tranquilizer—to calm you down.

6. Karate gives you increased body awareness, which helps you distinguish between nervous hunger and real hunger. Body awareness also helps you know

when you've eaten enough. Usually that's long before your second helping, and often before dessert.

7. Karate teaches you discipline. Many people find that they overeat in spite of themselves. They simply don't know how to change a bad habit. The discipline you learn from the *katas* will generalize to other areas of your life. You'll find you just naturally have more self-control than you've ever experienced before. You can apply it to your eating habits or to anything else.

In this chapter, I've shown you how karate can help your "outside"—your body. If doing something good for your body is your main reason for taking karate, that's fine. I think it's the most beneficial physical activity there is.

But remember, karate moves from the outside in. There isn't any way karate can affect your exterior without also affecting the internal you—the way you think, feel, and behave—because in karate, you unify your body and your mind. It's virtually impossible to improve yourself physically without increasing your mental fitness as well.

Chapter 6

Maximizing Your Mental Powers

Although karate is a discipline that you acquire through your body, you don't become a karateist in body only. Not if you make a true commitment to the art. When you master the *katas*, you inevitably and unconsciously—whether you try to or not—undergo profound *mental* changes that can dramatically alter your entire approach to life.

The knowledge that you get in your karate class will eventually generalize to all other aspects of your life. You will become a karateist in the way you speak, the way you think, the way you feel, and the way you act, not only while you're practicing the *katas*, but all the time—no matter what you're doing, where you're doing it, and who you're doing it with.

From Outside to Inside

The goal of most Western physical activities is simple: to perfect the execution of that activity. But karate's purpose is very different. Of course, initially, you must acquire the necessary skill. You must perfect the activity —master the *katas*. But that's only the beginning. Look at the goal of the *katas*, and you'll see what I mean. It's a twofold goal:

1. To teach you (through bodily movements) a flexible, practical philosophy of life
2. To unify your body and your mind (through mind and breath control), thereby *ensuring* that you incorporate the principles of that philosophy into your total being and make them truly your own.

More than any other physical activity, karate significantly affects your mental processes and influences the way you live your life. *I don't know one person who has truly committed himself or herself to karate who has not experienced deep, lasting mental changes.*

In what ways can karate change you? It can clarify your thinking, increase your awareness, lead you toward emotional maturity, broaden your attitudes, and improve your way of dealing with other people.

How *much* will it change you? That depends. Karate works on mental fitness just as it does on physical fitness: the worse shape you're in to start, the more spectacular the change.

Becoming Aware

Just as your body gets stronger with exercise, so does your mind. The *katas* require as much mental effort as physical effort, so they provide your mind with healthy exercise. You can actually increase your intellectual capabilities through karate. You can learn to think more logically and more clearly.

The *katas* teach you to summon and direct your *chi* toward mental tasks, as well as toward physical tasks. This means that you'll be better able to clear your mind of extraneous thoughts, you'll be better able to concentrate, and better able to remember important facts.

Of course, your mind doesn't only get stronger with exercise. It gets more flexible, too, and therefore more capable of solving difficult problems. If you've got a mind that bends, you'll be able to toss out an old approach if it doesn't work. You'll be more willing to try a new tack, even if no one's traveled that route before.

I can think of several students who feel they've "gotten smarter" through karate. One good example is Lester B. Les was just beginning his senior year of high school when I met him. Les had never done very well in school. "I barely made it from kindergarten to first grade," he once told me, only half joking. "And I've just been squeaking by ever since."

About three months after Les started karate, I happened to run into his father. He told me that Les had brought home his initial report card of the year. For the first time in his scholastic history, he was passing in every subject. He couldn't understand it.

I told him that learning karate wasn't very different

from learning anything else. It required mental effort and discipline. In the process, the student learned how to apply himself to any learning task.

"I think karate has turned on Les's mind in a way it's never been turned on before," I told his father. "And he doesn't click himself off when he leaves karate class. So he's more tuned in to what his teachers are saying."

When you learn karate, you don't only learn it with your body and your intellect, you learn it with your emotions as well. **Karate is designed to teach you to translate your emotions into a physical action.** When you perform a *kata*, you summon and intensify emotions at will, by using fantasy and breath control.

When you're practicing karate, you're purposefully exercising your emotions. You're not only expanding your capacity to feel deeply, but you're also developing a greater ability to identify your feelings and to detect subtle changes of emotion. You're becoming more aware.

Over the months, this awareness will become greater and greater. It will begin to generalize to all the other aspects of your life. You will become a more conscious person, whether you try to or not, whether you want to or not. And this awareness will continue to grow for as long as you study karate.

As time passes, you should come closer and closer to always knowing exactly how you're feeling, what mixture of emotions you're experiencing, at any given moment. You'll also probably be closer to knowing your precise feelings and attitudes when you have to make decisions— all sorts of decisions, little and big.

Karate will help you get more deeply in touch with your beliefs, your feelings, your ideas, and your opinions.

It will teach you new things about your tastes and appetites, your strengths and weaknesses, your talents and limitations. You'll very likely become more self-aware, better able to recognize your needs and administer to them.

I've seen many people who are afraid of becoming more aware of themselves. They're afraid of what they'll find out. But most people who take the chance discover that nothing terrible happens. In fact, their fears are worse than any reality.

Perhaps you have some fears about awareness. Perhaps you're afraid to experience your own powerful emotions because you think you'll lose control if you really let your feelings surface. Actually, an emotion that is repressed or tied down is potentially more dangerous or upsetting than one that is fully recognized and accepted. Repressed emotions don't atrophy or go away. When you overcontrol yourself, you don't kill your emotions. They are being constantly exercised—against the resistance you impose. So they get stronger, although your awareness doesn't. Then, maybe, one day all hell breaks loose, and you've no idea what's happened or how to handle it. The emotion has overwhelmed you and forced you out of control.

Remaining unaware may seem like a safe way to live, but it's really no way to deal with yourself or the rest of the world. Unaware people are far more *vulnerable* than they realize. They're more likely to suffer the damaging physical effects of stress diseases, and they're more likely to suffer mental breakdowns as well.

The shell most people surround themselves with really isn't as safe and protective as it seems. To develop your awareness, you must take some risks, by moving out of the shell. In the long run, your own awareness is the best protection you can possibly have. And through it comes your greatest opportunity for satisfaction in life.

This doesn't mean that once you become aware, the only thing you'll care about is you. In a karate class, you're working with other people and their emotions at the same time you're dealing with your own. This should not only make you more sensitive to others, but it should also teach you something about how you relate to the rest of the world. Since you don't live in a vacuum, genuine self-awareness must include awareness of others and awareness of yourself in relationship to your environment. This will contribute to your adaptability and help make it possible for you to anticipate and deal with change.

Today, an increasing number of people are feeling dissatisfied with the way their lives are going. More and more people are visiting psychiatrists, psychologists, and counselors because they feel they need help. More and more people are buying more and more books on psychotherapy, in hopes that by reading them they'll be better able to help themselves. Most professionals agree that before a person can effectively change himself or his life, he must become more aware. Helping you to build awareness is one of karate's most valuable gifts.

David V. is a good example. When he started taking karate, he was a thirty-five-year-old accountant who'd just been made senior partner in a medium-size, highly respected accounting firm. Except for a founding partner, David was the youngest senior partner in the firm's fifty-year history.

David didn't realize that he had his doubts about accounting until he became senior partner. Then he noticed that everyone else seemed more excited over his success than he did. He was working longer hours, spending less time with the family, less time outdoors, and more time sitting in a chair.

A friend suggested David come to karate classes with him. It would be good exercise and a nice diversion from the paper work. David gave it a try. He wasn't wildly enthusiastic at first, but, encouraged by his friend to keep it up, David eventually was hooked. As the months went by, David began to feel increasingly resentful toward his job—not the work, necessarily, but the sedentary, indoor life he was forced to live.

"I'm not so sure I want to be an accountant at all anymore," David once told me.

"But you're very successful at it," I said.

"Yes, and that's nice. I like having enough money to buy what I need and most of what I want. What I don't like is having to spend ten or twelve hours a day doing something I don't enjoy. Come to think of it, that's what I've been doing for fifteen years."

It wasn't until six months later that David told me he'd bought a half-interest in a nursery. "I'd been getting pretty friendly with the owners," David said. "I took up gardening as a hobby a couple of months after I started karate. And I found out that one partner—the older one—was retiring to Florida. I offered to buy him out, and they both agreed."

"What about the accounting business?" I asked.

"I resigned." David was smiling broadly. "My parents were in an uproar, and it was a low blow to my wife's prestige too. But really, she didn't take it terribly hard. We can get along on a smaller income for a little while.

"But the most important thing is the way I feel. I

finally found out what I wanted, figured out how to get it, and I'm enjoying my life a hundred percent more because of it."

I asked David if he thought taking karate had helped him make the big decision.

"Oh, there's no doubt about it," he said. "That's when I first became aware that I was unhappy with the accounting field. If I hadn't started karate, I might still be there. And maybe I wouldn't have found out I hated it until I actually got to be chairman of the board. By then, it would probably have been too late.

"Karate helped me know myself better."

Building Self-Esteem

When you become more mentally disciplined and more aware through karate, you discover discipline and awareness are capabilities that you—and nearly everyone else—already have. You are forced to awaken these inner resources to learn karate, which in turn exercises and expands them.

The same goes for self-confidence. Belief in yourself is one of the most important inner resources any individual has. Unfortunately, it's often very elusive. But karate can help you develop it.

Ironically, when you begin karate, you may notice that whatever confidence you thought you had is shaken. That's because, in karate class, where there is actual physical contact, you come face to face not only with your skills but also with your fear. Looking yourself squarely in the eye this way is the first step toward developing real self-confidence.

As you progress in karate, you not only increase your skill, but you also develop a greater and greater ability to perform under stress. Gradually you become more and more confident. This increasing confidence is not superficial. In karate, there's no way to escape the reality of your emotions. Whether you want to or not, whether you try to or not, you will experience a gut-level change in the way you feel about yourself. Your self-esteem will grow, affecting everything you do.

Once you have a more positive self-image, you don't have to fool yourself about your capabilities. You'll be better able to evaluate and accept both your strengths and your limitations. Your self-compassion will grow. You'll begin to like yourself, despite your human frailties.

Self-worth is not based upon external achievements. It comes from within. Practically speaking, a sense of self-esteem gives you the freedom to try many new things because it lessens your fear of failure. You'll begin to see that your intrinsic value as a human being doesn't decrease with each failure or increase with each success.

When you feel better about yourself, you are less likely to feel threatened by change. You become more open to new ideas. When you feel positive about yourself, you're also more likely to feel positive about other people and about life. You're more able to experience positive emotions, like joy and pleasure and satisfaction and love.

Low self-esteem is the prime cause of neurotic behavior, which is compulsive and destructive, and is almost always triggered by negative emotions like anger, hostility, anxiety, frustration, depression, and despair. These emotions usually arise when you feel threatened by change or when you are unprepared to deal with change. The change or threat (stress) releases energy (*chi*) which, if you have a low self-image, you will use in a negative way.

Depending on who you are, you'll either express your negative feelings by lashing out at someone else or by turning inward on yourself. Either way, your energy is dissipated, wasted. And that hurts you—if not physically then psychologically.

But as your awareness increases and you begin to feel more confident and your self-image begins to change, you'll be more able to accept and adapt to change. You'll begin to experience fewer and fewer negative emotions. A person who feels good about himself is more naturally inclined to use his energy positively, to his best end.

That doesn't mean you'll never feel negative emotions once you develop more self-esteem. Of course you will; everyone does. But when you do, you'll be far less likely to respond to them neurotically—to explode with them or to wallow in them. You'll be much more capable of converting that energy into something positive and directing it to a more productive goal. You'll find, also, that you experience fewer wide mood shifts. You'll feel on a more even keel, more stable.

I have seen several people undergo very dramatic changes since they started taking karate—improvements in their self-image that literally saved their lives.

Paul C. was twenty-two years old when he started studying with me. He was an extremely anxious person, had been ever since he was a young child. As Paul grew up, he tried to work off much of his anxiety with exercise. He became a good athlete and might have had a career in track or swimming had he not been drafted.

After he returned from Vietnam, he enrolled in my school.

When I first met him, Paul was very depressed. One look at him and I knew something was wrong. He was barely holding himself together. Except for running a few miles every day and coming to karate class four nights a week, he couldn't do anything.

I felt that if Paul stuck with karate he would come out of it. Sure enough, little by little, Paul began to develop his awareness and raise his self-confidence.

Now, four years later, Paul isn't the same person he was when he first walked into the school. He no longer mumbles and stammers, but speaks articulately, though softly. And he has been accepted into a sales training program at a business machine company.

Of course, everyone who studies karate may not undergo such spectacular changes as Paul. Chances are, you're not in such dire need. But karate can give you confidence in areas where you might not have had any before—a confidence that might enable you to try something different.

The Path to Inner Peace

Most people who are at least aware enough to know they'd like to change often don't have any idea of what to do in order to change. Usually they feel something like this: "I'm not happy with myself. I think I should be . . ." Then they select some model of what they think is right, and try to force themselves to fit it. They go to war with themselves.

Perhaps you've gone to war with yourself from time

to time. Maybe you've felt that you are really two—or more—people. Or that if you let the "real you" take over, no one would recognize you. Or maybe that the kind of life you're living doesn't reflect any of your inner feelings or fulfill your inner needs.

Well, maybe you're right and maybe you're wrong. There's really no way you're going to find out for sure until you stop telling yourself *how you should be* and start asking yourself *how you are*.

In karate, you learn about yourself, by getting in touch with your emotions. As your awareness develops, how you should be becomes obvious. You should be the way you are.

Once you truly know yourself and develop your ability to accept yourself as you are, you don't have to fight yourself so much. Your internal conflicts begin to resolve themselves. You will find that you are changing. You are not trying to change—to become someone you're not (someone you think you should be). Instead, you're becoming more of who you are.

As you become more conscious of yourself, you'll develop in a direction that's right and natural for you. You'll begin to feel increasingly at peace with yourself, which in turn creates a climate for further growth. And while you are changing and growing yourself, your way of dealing with other people should also change and improve.

Improving Relationships

The most crucial part of your karate instruction comes when you begin to relate your own moves to the moves of another person. By constantly dealing with yourself *and* with other individuals on an intimate physical and emotional level, you are forced to sharpen further not only your self-awareness but your senses as well.

You learn to observe other people closely, to watch them, to listen to them, to touch them. You begin to distinguish small signals, very subtle signs that most other people never become aware of either in themselves or in others. And you learn to analyze these signals very quickly—automatically after a while. You'll notice how a person speaks, whether he draws out his words or clips them. You'll notice whether his voice is high or low. Does he look you in the eye? What do his eyes tell you? These and hundreds of other tiny details will provide you with valuable clues. Eventually you may become so alert that you can predict what another person will do in karate class. And you'll begin to know how he feels, just as you know how you feel.

Your awareness of others will increase with your own growing self-awareness and with your continued interaction with the other members of your karate class. Whether you want it to or not, whether you try to make it happen or not, your awareness of others will generalize and will affect all your other relationships.

You should feel less different and separate from the rest of the human race, perhaps less lonely. You'll feel increased empathy and compassion for others because you'll feel it for yourself. You'll become more and more sensitive to the needs and emotions of others, just as you become more sensitive to your own feelings and needs.

You will also find that you can communicate better with other people. How often do you find yourself tuning out in the middle of a conversation, trying to think of what you're going to say rather than truly listening to the other person? Chances are that nearly half of what other people say to you is lost. And probably, half of what you say to them is lost too. There is no real exchange of information going on in most conversations.

Most of the time—pathetically, I think—people aren't really responding to each other but to their own preconceived ideas. They really aren't able to make contact. In karate, you'll learn how to empty your mind of preconceptions and to respond to the here and now. When you can do this, you will find that you are making genuine contact with others.

Even those people who are very aware and who usually communicate rather well have difficulty achieving more than a rare moment or two of genuine emotional intimacy with another person. As you continue with karate, you'll find that these moments become extended and that they happen more frequently. As your awareness and self-confidence grow, you'll become less fearful in your relations with other people. You'll have more freedom to be spontaneous, friendly, warm and honest. By honesty, I mean a willingness and ability to tell other people your feelings. When you're able to express yourself continually, by being direct and honest, you become less provokable, less defensive, less violent. You have much better self-control, yet you are not holding yourself back or restricting your flow of emotion.

And you're not the only one who'll feel better when you can deal honestly with others. By being direct and responding to them with your real feelings, you put them at ease.

You will find, as you become more capable of relating

to other people on a more honest level, that more people like you for what you really are, rather than for what you might be pretending to be. Not only will you have more confidence in yourself, but you'll also have more confidence and trust in your friends. In this atmosphere, more rewarding relationships can flourish. And karate can help you create it.

In karate, you will become friends with your emotions, learning what they are, why they are, and how to control them. From here, it's only one more step to realizing that you're very much like everyone else—at least in your essential emotional responses. In gaining an insight into your own emotions, needs and responses, you will also gain an insight into the emotions, needs, and responses of others. And the better you know yourself, the better you'll know the rest of humanity.

How Karate Helps Your Everyday Life

Once you change the way you think and feel and the way you relate to other people, you're bound to make some corresponding changes in the way you live your life every single day. The closer you come to being an aware, unified individual, the more your life will be a reflection of you.

What does everyday life consist of? Mostly, it's a set of patterns or routines, *very much like kata.* What can go wrong? Our behavior can become so mechanical that we ignore the pleasures of subtle change. We become too rigid, let our imaginations atrophy, feel bored, lose our efficiency.

One of the first things many people notice after they've

studied karate for a while is that they approach their everyday lives a little more creatively. They vary their routines just enough so that they feel more alive, less restless and bored. You realize that even within the discipline of your everyday tasks, or *kata*, you can become more creative and aware.

In addition to the patterns we follow as we go through our days, we are also all subjected to stress, more or less depending upon who we are and how we're living. Most people react badly to stress. They're overwhelmed by change and frightened by the prospect of it. You can become more comfortable with the idea of change through karate. As you begin to make little changes here and there, you'll start to realize you can look forward to change, instead of fearing it.

Of course, no matter how much you appreciate and enjoy change, all changes are not pleasant. Some can be very troublesome. Karate also prepares you to deal more effectively with those changes that are disturbing. Karate teaches you to anticipate change, too, which often enables you to turn it to your advantage.

Change often makes us feel out of control. Instead of moving with the change, we try to resist it, to regain control—and we block our flow of energy or *chi*. This starts a vicious cycle of nonproductivity. We lose control, try to regain it, worry, fail to produce, worry more and produce even less.

If you're a businessman or woman trying to earn a living, or an artist who is blocked, or a student who can't study, this is very damaging indeed. Unless you can direct and use the energy stress releases, you are likely to suffer harmful mental and physical effects.

Karate teaches you to empty your mind. It gives you

the capability of taking an instant vacation from your desire to produce, from your fears about being unable to produce, from your uneasiness about your abilities, from your mechanical habits. When you can clear your mind, every experience you have becomes fresh again. You'll see things differently, and you'll be more able to put things together in new ways. You'll begin to see the substance of your problems, rather than focusing on specific content or on old solutions that you know don't work.

Let's say you were turned down for a promotion. Instead of fretting and worrying about why you were passed up, you'll be better able to spot the qualities that worked for the other guy. You'll be more likely to improve your performance on the job, instead of being so upset that you can't work at all.

Maybe you're an artist or a writer who is blocked. Instead of telling yourself you have no talent and becoming more depressed about your inability to work, chances are you'll be able to find new solutions to your problems. Or you'll be more likely to generate new ideas.

What if you're a student who suddenly finds his grades falling because of an inability to concentrate or study? By emptying your mind and letting yourself rest, you'll have a chance to renew your interest in the subjects you're studying. Once you open yourself up, some aspect in your schooling will probably begin to appeal to you.

I know a famous story about a fifteenth-century Zen painter that will illustrate the value of being able to empty your mind. This artist was struggling to master the technique of painting on silk with ink. The silk was so absorbent that once the painter set his brush down, he could not lift it until he was completely finished painting. So he had to work quickly and flawlessly, controlling the flow of ink with precision. The slightest imperfection ruined the painting and forced him to start all over again.

Day after day the artist tried to complete a painting only to find himself lifting his brush before he'd finished. He ruined silk after silk. He began to worry. Would he ever master the technique? Eventually it occurred to him that worry wasn't going to help him paint. In fact, it was preventing him from accomplishing his goals. He began to realize that his problem wasn't really technique. He'd mastered that. His trouble was in his head. He knew how to paint in a single continuous stroke, he knew how to control the brush and the flow of ink. But he didn't know how to control his own self-defeating thoughts.

One day he set out some incense on either side of his work table. Then he washed his hands and his inkwell. Instead of allowing himself to wonder whether or not he would succeed that day, he sat down quietly, as if he were about to welcome a distinguished guest. And he waited patiently.

His vision of what to paint arrived. The artist was able to perceive his idea clearly because his mind was free of other thoughts. He spontaneously set to work, letting his energy flow just as freely as the ink flowed from his brush. And he completed his painting, which turned out to be one of the masterpieces of the day.

Karate also teaches you to approach life from a *dynamically balanced position*. You can respond more spontaneously to change. You can learn to move, without losing your balance and falling all over yourself—mentally, as well as physically.

For most people, feeling secure involves staying the

same. Change—both internal change and external change —is risky, so almost everyone resists it in order to feel secure. But change is a fact of life. The Greek philosopher Heraclitus, who lived in the sixth century B.C., believed that there was no permanent reality but the reality of change. Permanency was an illusion, he felt: "You never step into the same river twice." Just as the river is always flowing and changing, so is life. We cannot make ourselves more secure by resisting change. We would only be waging a losing battle.

Karate helps you to maintain control during change, and it teaches you how to accept change more readily. Through dynamic balance, you can learn to feel secure in spite of change. More than that, through breath control karate teaches you how to make use of the stress that inevitably comes with change, how to turn your fears and anxieties and tensions to your advantage instead of letting them hinder your ability to function, how to use and direct the energy that stress generates.

No matter what kind of stress situation you find yourself in, karate may be able to help you. And keep in mind that stress isn't only having a high-pressure job or feeling a financial pinch. Stress comes from any kind of change, and no one who is alive is immune to it.

If you're a parent, you have to deal with your growing (changing) children, as well as with society's changing views on child rearing; if you're a student, you are still growing up and must prepare for the day when you graduate as well as for changes in your courses from term to term or changes in your educational goals; if you're in the business world, you have to deal with competition that is constantly coming into the marketplace as well as with changes within your organization.

If your best friend moves away, that's change. If you date someone for the first time, that's change. If you take a vacation, that's change. It's also change if your alarm doesn't go off one morning—or if you get to work ahead of your usual time. If your shoelace breaks or if you spill your coffee, that's change. So is inheriting unexpected money.

Even pleasurable or beneficial changes are sometimes hard to deal with, because we're so taken by surprise that we can hardly react appropriately. We don't know how to make the most of our opportunities. But with karate, you can often make any kind of change work in your favor. Even the ones that look negative frequently provide hidden opportunities.

Karate also helps you live from day to day by teaching you something about your relationship with the rest of the world. When you can begin to see the outside as an extension of yourself, and yourself as a part of everything else, you're more likely to become an active, effective part of the whole.

Karate can help prepare you to deal with all kinds of events: losing your job or getting a new one; having your first child or marrying off your last; selling your stocks at a loss or making a killing in the market; hearing from your doctor that you're in great shape or that you've got to watch your heart; graduating from college or facing retirement.

But giving you an easier time dealing with events isn't the only day-to-day benefit karate offers. By enlarging your perspective and increasing your insight, karate can also help you relate better to other people. This is perhaps one of karate's most satisfying benefits.

The ability to deal well with others is one of the most sought-after qualities in the business world, but this isn't the only place it counts. Most people have families and friends as well as business associates. Almost everyone longs for social acceptance. Everyone needs rewarding relationships with others.

Many people I know who once feared change also felt threatened by other people and avoided forming close relationships. Just as karate can help improve your attitude toward change, so it can make a difference in how you feel about other people.

One of my students told me he'd become more sociable since he began taking karate. "I used to be very aloof and cold to other people," he said. "Now I'm more friendly. I have to admit that I used to be frightened of other people. I thought I disliked them, but now I know that wasn't the case."

Karate has helped me personally—and helped hundreds of people I know—to appreciate more fully the small pleasures of daily living. It's also helped me learn to deal with the little disappointments that are an inevitable part of living. If I can't find a way to use these unpleasant changes to my own advantage, at least I'm not thrown by them.

But I think karate can do much more than increase the pleasure you get from each day you're alive. I also feel that it can help ensure a vital and rewarding future. Karate can help keep you young and flexible. It can build awareness and self-confidence. Karate can make you more valuable to yourself, and thereby help you to make a greater contribution to the others around you. And it can help you achieve the freedom that comes from being able to move with change.

Chapter 7

An Enriched Sex Life

One of the things people fear most is a loss of sexual vitality. It's very threatening to lose your sexual interest and abilities. Yet many recent studies have shown there's no reason a person's capacity to enjoy sex should diminish as the years go by. If you do everything you can to stay healthy, to remain physically and mentally flexible as you move through life, you can continue to function sexually regardless of age.

Karate will help keep all your systems operative. It will help you look, feel, and behave as you would if you were actually younger, making all aspects of living—including sex—more pleasurable and meaningful.

Sex and the Ancients

Through the years, karate has been influenced by every imaginable attitude toward sex. Karateists have been everything from celibates to hedonists. But most martial artists have conducted their sex lives according to the prevailing mores of the time, in accord with the customs of their particular culture or culture group. (And that's as true today as it was thousands of years ago.)

Some of the early martial artists, particularly those who strived for spiritual enlightenment, practiced abstinence. Their reasons were as much pragmatic as moralistic. They believed that sexual relations would use up valuable *chi*. They feared that having sex would rob them of the strength and energy they needed to perform various physical feats and to reach a state of *nirvana*.

Taoism and Sex

The idea of losing precious life energy through sexual acts is a popular Taoist concept. So is the notion that sexual partners give each other a valuable gift of *chi* during sexual intercourse. The Taoists felt that the *chi*, the essence of life, was contained within the *yin* and the *yang* and was released during orgasm.

The Tao spiritual leaders wanted to retain as much of their *chi* as they could. But they also felt that the more *chi* they could get from a person of the opposite sex, the closer they would become to being fully complete, energized and enlightened individuals. So they did not abstain from sex.

According to the *yin/yang* concept, male and female are mutually dependent. They are opposites and complements. Each sex strives to complete itself by joining with the other. Thus, for the Taoist, sex promoted a harmonization of *yin* and *yang* and contributed to a person's overall vitality and longevity.

The Chinese Taoists weren't the only people who believed that good health, longevity, and vitality were linked to sexual activity. The Hindu religion in India took a similar view, which eventually came to be expressed in the *Kamasutra*. The *Kamasutra* was written in Sanskrit, and scholars date it sometime between the fourth and seventh centuries A.D.—within two hundred years of Bodhidharma's arrival in China. Most people today think of the *Kamasutra* as the first "marriage manual." Actually, it was more of a Hindu physical fitness program than a sex-instruction book.

Finding Sensual Fulfillment

The Western view of sex never quite paralleled that of the East. It was not so firmly or formally linked to vitality or longevity. Religion had little to say about it, except in the moral sense, or as the means to procreativity. In fact, until recently, our culture generally held the view that sex—especially in excess—could be debilitating. This idea was especially prevalent in athletic circles, where it was felt that sex could diminish performance.

This notion seems to be undergoing revision today. Fewer and fewer athletes subscribe to this idea, to judge from their public statements. However, as a trainer, I'd say that moderation is in order, especially shortly before important games or events.

Today, many modern karateists believe that karate can improve a person's sexual self-confidence, loosen some inhibitions, and dampen sexual worries. And there are several reasons for this belief.

Karate makes you more sexually fit. By making you more physically fit in general, karate also makes you more sexually fit. Sex is a physical activity, which you'll be more able to perform and enjoy if you are in good shape just as you'll be able to perform and enjoy any other physical activity more when you're in condition for it.

When you're physically fit, you don't tire as easily. You've got more energy for everything, including sex. Whatever you do is more fun, more rewarding, when you're in shape. You're a more vital, more feeling individual.

Being completely physically fit also affects your mental state, and this is especially important when it comes to sex. Physical fitness increases not only your capabilities, but also your self-confidence.

Moreover, when you're physically fit, you feel healthier and you look your best—and you know it. This helps you feel more sexually desirable, and, therefore, more desirous. You become more aware of your sexual feelings.

Karate can increase your ability to fantasize. Today, most psychologists and psychiatrists—and many non-professionals as well—agree that fantasy can play an important role in your enjoyment of sex. It can help energize you if you're tired. It can help turn you on if the situation isn't as exciting or as novel as you'd like. And if you can turn yourself on, you're more likely to turn on your partner as well.

To the karateist, fantasy is a valuable tool—not only

with regard to sex. In karate, we learn to create images in our minds. We picture situations and put ourselves into them. This enables us to create stress as well.

If you've never been able to have fantasies, karate will help you. You won't learn how to create sexual fantasies in karate class, but you will learn how to fantasize about other things. This will give you an ability that you can use for sexual purposes, if you desire.

Karate can increase your sensuality and lower your inhibitions. Through karate, you will learn to respond more readily to stimuli. Karate will help develop your senses and increase your perceptual abilities. This is particularly useful when it comes to sex.

Karate training also lowers your inhibitions—or rather, gives you the ability to loosen up when you want to. One of the most common inhibitions has to do with touching other people. And I'm not speaking here about sexual touching, particularly, but about any touching. In karate class, we learn to touch other people. We learn to feel comfortable relating in a physical (but nonsexual) way. We lose our fear of touching another person and of being touched.

Karate can rekindle your interest in sex. Karate teaches you to free yourself from boredom in any aspect of your life, including sex. It shows you how to look at life from a different perspective. It helps you use your imagination and think creatively. For these reasons, karate can help you renew your interest in sex. Sometimes that's necessary, especially when you've had the same sexual partner for many years. Doing the same things over and over again with the same person can become stale—no matter how much you care for the person and no matter how much you like what you're doing.

Through karate, however, you can find new interest

in long-established activities, or those that have become little more than habit. When you apply this ability to sex, you can increase not only your own pleasure, but also the pleasure of your partner.

Karate can improve your relations with your sexual partner. Just as karate can improve all aspects of your relations with other people, so it can also improve your ability to relate sexually. Karate helps you to develop an awareness of others. It helps you to feel empathy for your friends and associates. It makes you more comfortable with other people, and more able to communicate with them. This new ability, when applied to your sexual life, can make you a more sensitive, more considerate, more aware sexual partner.

Karate can help you build sexual self-confidence. Every man knows there's nothing worse for his sex life than worrying about his ability to perform. Yet fear of failure is probably the most common cause of sexual impotency. Women have similar problems with frigidity.

Karate can help in this area because it gives you a way to deal with all kinds of stress, including fears of sexual inadequacy. If you're a karateist, you'll be unlikely to waste your energy with self-defeating thoughts. And you won't assume that lack of success on some occasions means that you're doomed to fail every time. Instead, you will be able to use your *chi* toward some constructive end.

Maybe you'll just direct your energy into emptying your mind of conscious thoughts—ridding yourself of your fears and your intense desire to produce. Sometimes, "letting go" is all you'll have to do. Or you can put your energy into a fantasy, or direct it toward appreciating the stimuli—your partner, your surroundings, the various sensual feelings you're having. Anything can happen when you're not overwhelmed by your concern for your performance.

As long as you're only thinking and worrying about yourself, you won't be able to please your partner to the maximum. Without sexual self-confidence, it's nearly impossible to be warm, loving, giving, or responsive. Karate can give you what you need.

Karate can help you control the physical aspects of sex. Perhaps more than any other human activity, sex depends on a unity of mind and body. It is the separate activity of each of these aspects that is responsible for most sexual difficulties. One of karate's key goals, however, is to join mind and body, so that they operate as one. In the sexual sphere, this will enable you to express your real feelings physically, to integrate your needs and desires with your actions.

When you study karate, you learn to control your physiological responses with your breath. If you want to energize or excite yourself, you can—through karate breathing techniques. The same techniques will aid you to calm yourself, to lower your level of excitation. This unity of mind and body, added to the control of physical response, will make you able to express yourself sexually and control your sexual responses in a manner that will maximize pleasure, both for you and for your sexual partner.

Living the Sensual Life

Unfortunately, many people only enjoy the excitement and sensations of extreme vitality during sexual encounter. This need not be the case. Your whole life can be as full of that special energized quality, that certain glowing warmth that you've always attached to sexual feelings. With karate, your every act can be given new vitality and energy—of just the sort you formerly thought limited to sexual activity.

The ancients—as well as contemporary visionaries—have spoken of man's ability to transform his generally dulled conscious self, in both the mental and physical sense, into new dimensions of energy and vitality. They've described a life lived at the forward edge of sensitivity and awareness, a life that many people have experienced only during sexual activity. Karate can help you experience these feelings in all your waking moments, regardless of their content, thereby leading you to new levels of consciousness both in the physical and the mental sense. It can help you lead a life that is, in the best sense, constantly sensual.

Chapter 8

The Ultimate Self-Defense

This chapter will not make you a self-defense expert, but it can help you to deal better with some kinds of attack situations. It can give you the karateist's approach to self-defense, tell you something about the way he thinks when he's attacked, and describe the kinds of skills he has. If you study karate, you'll learn the finer points of its principles, the details of applying them in a self-defense situation, and the exceptions to all the rules.

Winning Through Nonviolence

When you think of self-defense, you probably think of fighting and violence. In karate, self-defense begins long before the fighting starts. It begins with *avoiding violence whenever possible.*

One of my students put it rather well. He said, "I used to find myself in a brawl every so often. I could never understand why it happened, and I always felt terrible afterward. I thought it was because I lost a lot. When I first started taking karate, I thought it would help me win more fights. But now I know that my greatest victory is in not fighting at all. Now I can walk away from a fight. And there's no dishonor in refusing a useless fight. I certainly didn't get what I expected from karate. I got something much better."

Even if you study karate for only a brief time—not long enough to become an accomplished fighter—you will learn something about the art of self-protection. You will learn something about the nature of conflict, the nature of violence, and the value of nonviolence. You'll learn something about the part you might play in creating or avoiding violence.

A true karateist knows that violence really can't settle anything. If you provoke violence, you may be hurting someone else, but it's not likely that by doing so you're protecting yourself. Violence only increases your chances of getting hurt. If you start violence, or respond to violence with unnecessary violence, you'll find yourself trapped in an endless chain of aggression. Nobody escapes from this cycle unharmed.

In karate, you learn the value of nonviolence by being exposed to violence—by enacting situations of conflict in karate class. You learn to see the anger, frustration, and fear in the people around you and in yourself. And you begin to understand that no one can endure a fight without being hurt—either physically or emotionally. Through karate you will come to realize that violence is not only pointless, it is inevitably damaging as well.

The violent individual shows a lack of intelligence and a lack of self-awareness. He feels angry and insecure, and instead of facing his problems directly, he takes his troubles out on others around him. The person who forces violence, who lures you into a fight, is trying to test himself against you. Unless you are equally insecure, or equally unintelligent, or equally unaware, you won't take his bait.

Despite my familiarity with violence, I try never to get involved with it. I've seen too much of it to believe it's a valid way of resolving problems. Every so often, someone who has heard of my ability as a karateist will challenge me. I won't accept. The challenger ostensibly wants to know which of us is the better fighter. But I know exactly what I'm capable of—so there's no reason for me to test myself against anyone else.

Fighting isn't going to change what I can do or what the challenger can do. It won't increase my self-confidence if I win. And it won't lower it if I don't.

I know how pain feels. I know it so well that I can tell when another person is hurting. Will I be able to justify my actions, or was the situation avoidable?

Karate has taught me that the best master is one who never gets into a fight. He has learned the total art of karate. I've learned that it's crazy to walk down a dark street in a bad neighborhood, no matter how skilled a fighter I am. I've learned that I don't have to take unnecessary risks, or accept challenges, or test myself, or try to prove myself. These are among the first lessons in karate.

Avoiding a fight isn't always as simple as saying no to a direct challenge or just making sure you stay out of harm's way. People who haven't studied karate, who haven't learned the principle of nonconfrontation, sometimes find themselves being baited into violent encounters before they know what's happening to them.

Karate will help you learn to anticipate violence before it occurs, by building your awareness. If you can anticipate, you can also often avoid. As a karateist, you'll be able to assess nearly any situation with a high degree of accuracy. You'll be more likely to see conflicting personalities at odds, feel undercurrents of pride and anger. You'll frequently spot the elements that can lead to violence, watch them build, and predict—sometimes with incredible accuracy—the exact moment of eruption. One would hope, having done that, you'll leave the scene. You will have evaluated, anticipated, and avoided.

Very often, I can tell when other people are about to burst out in anger, even before they themselves know they're going to do it. Not long ago, for example, I stopped into a bar to have a beer with a few of my students. As we sat at our table, I could see all the conditions for a big brawl building up.

Several men at the bar were talking loud and fast, swigging their drinks down quickly. In that bar that night were all the ingredients for a classic barroom fight.

As the tension started to build, it began to affect my students. They started feeling uneasy. "What's the matter with you?" one nervous brown belt asked me. "How can you just sit here calmly when the whole bar is going to explode in a minute?"

We stayed at the table and I slowly sipped my beer. I

tried to get my companions to do the same, but they
were too jumpy.

On the other side of the room, a few halfhearted
punches were thrown. My students were on the edge of
their chairs. All of a sudden, I sensed that the whole
room was going to break up, so I put down my glass and
said it was time to go. As we were walking out the door,
I looked behind me and saw that the table we'd been
sitting at had been turned over. It looked as though
every person in the place was involved in the fight.

Evaluating Yourself

Being aware of your *own* feelings and moods is as
much a part of nonconfrontation as analyzing a situation
and evaluating how others will respond. An accomplished karateist usually recognizes even the slightest
shift in his moods. He can normally stay in touch with
his emotions as they build and deal with them as the
level of intensity increases, remaining in control of his
behavior.

Let me give you an example of how even a nonviolent
individual can find himself suddenly involved in a violent scene simply because he lacks the self-awareness to
avoid it.

Put yourself in this situation. You're driving to work
one hot summer morning, and the traffic is a little heavier
than usual. Lots of people are beeping their horns,
changing lanes frequently, driving carelessly and rudely.
As you get closer to the office, you begin to think about
the pile of papers waiting for you on your desk—work

you should have finished up yesterday. You start wondering what you can tell the boss, and you start sweating.

As you approach your office building, you spot a legal parking place on the street. "Great," you think. "That should give me an extra ten minutes to get some work done."

You line up your car with the car in front of your space and shift into reverse. You check your rearview mirror and see, to your amazement, that a small foreign car has pulled into your space from behind.

Out you jump like a cannonball, filled with indignation. As the other guy is locking his car door, you walk up to him, furious now, and you soon find yourself involved in a fist fight, almost before you know it.

Why? What really happened? You usually don't even get annoyed over little things, let alone enraged. Why did you suddenly hit this guy?

You didn't get into a fight with this fellow because he stole your parking place, that's for sure. You lost your temper because you didn't know just how upset you were about the heat, the traffic, the rude and careless driving going on all around you, the leftover work you had to do. Not being aware of your feelings, you were unprepared to deal with them.

Let's see how you might improve your reaction to the same situation. All during the drive to work, you would have been aware of your response to the hostile environment. You wouldn't have tried to deny that the heat, the traffic, etc., were all getting to you. You would have recognized the first subtle signs of tension, frustration, anger.

Because you'd recognized and accepted your feelings,

their power to overwhelm you—to make you explode uncontrollably—would have been greatly diminished. More than likely you would have felt irritated, but not furious, when someone else got your space.

The karateist learns to recognize the first subtle signs of emotion, especially feelings that he might otherwise express as anger when things aren't going just right. The karateist is aware of what he is reacting to, how he is reacting, and why he is experiencing a particular reaction. This is an extremely important ability in avoiding conflict.

All around us we see conflicts occurring simply because people first sense their anger when it's too strong to control, instead of feeling and identifying it earlier, in its first stages. Sensing your emotions won't necessarily keep you from wanting to blow up from time to time. But a karate-sharp awareness will give you the ability to deal with your anger and excitement in a safe, non-violent way. As a karateist, you know the danger of provoking a violent response in someone else. This is why a karateist's self-evaluation also includes knowing just how he is affecting the people around him.

Whenever you have a conversation with another individual, you are creating an impression. If you have no idea what that impression is, you leave yourself open to the possibility of misunderstanding, anger, even violence. So karate not only teaches you to monitor your own feelings, but also to evaluate automatically the reactions of the people to whom you are relating at any given moment. As a karateist—and a conversationalist—you watch the expressions and gestures of the person you're talking to. You listen to his tone of voice as well as his words. If he misunderstands anything you say and takes offense, you will know it immediately. This way, conversational misunderstandings and disagreements won't build into physical confrontations.

Remember, the karateist doesn't initiate or provoke violence. Karate has taught him that even a little violence is too much.

Dealing with Violence

Violence *is* part of our society. No matter how skilled you are at avoiding violence, it may not always be possible. You may someday find yourself in an up-against-the-wall situation where you really have to fight for your life. At that moment, your ability to defend yourself will be all that matters.

The possibility that you could be personally threatened by a violent attack is reality. You can't ignore it. The ability to recognize and deal effectively with the reality of violence is a vital part of karate. It was to deal effectively with violence that karate's fighting moves first developed thousands of years ago.

Most people think of karate combat as Oriental street fighting or an Oriental boxing match with feet instead of with fists. In reality, karate combat is a far more efficient means of self-defense than either boxing or street fighting, which provide haphazard, uncertain and unreliable protection in comparison.

One reason for karate's superiority is that it alone teaches its practitioners how to deal with fear. That's the key emotion you'll feel when you're facing violence. If you're overwhelmed by your fear, you won't be able to function well enough to protect yourself.

Stress is a physical reaction to any kind of change. Fear is one kind of stress. It's what we experience when we're threatened. At its most intense, it's probably the most extreme stress reaction we can experience. Most people panic when faced with intense fear. They're not only afraid of the danger from their attacker, but they're also afraid of their inability to control their own behavior.

When you panic, you may shake all over without being able to stop yourself. You breathe quickly and shallowly. You're probably confused. Your reflexes most likely slow down. Your strength probably diminishes. You tire very quickly. And you may literally be paralyzed—unable to take any action at all.

If you've ever been in the armed services and seen combat, you may have experienced any or all of these reactions. If you've ever been mugged, raped, or otherwise threatened with bodily harm, then you've probably known what it's like to be intensely afraid.

How does karate help you to deal with the fear you'll inevitably feel if you're attacked? I mentioned earlier that in karate class, you'll learn to call forth your emotions by using your powers of concentration. By working with your fear over and over, by making yourself feel afraid and by becoming familiar with that experience, by dealing with that feeling again and again, you learn to be more comfortable with it. You learn to accept your fear, to recognize it. It will become a friend. This is the first step to keeping your wits and staying panic-free when you're threatened.

Being free from panic doesn't mean being free from fear. In fact, if you're a karateist, you need your fear. Remember, it's your stress reaction that triggers your *chi*. In other words, your fear gives you the energy to defend yourself.

Karate teaches you to empty your mind of conscious thought and to unify your mind and your body. The better you can do these things, the better you'll be able to direct and unify that energy so you're more able to respond quickly, automatically, and efficiently when you're attacked. Through karate, you'll learn to focus more and more of your entire being toward a single goal. In the case of an attack, that goal is to protect yourself.

There is no other means of self-defense that prepares you to deal with fear (and other kinds of stress) as systematically as does karate. When you learn to make use of stress through karate training, you'll be developing an ability that you can call upon at any time. Eventually, if you truly commit yourself to the art, you can learn to use stress to supercharge yourself—to mobilize your energy totally and so concentrate it that you can perform feats of strength and agility that would be incredible in normal circumstances.

They're not incredible. Karate helps you liberate tremendous physical and mental resources. When you're operating in a supercharged state, you're drawing upon all your resources at once. You're functioning at nearly total efficiency, so your normal abilities are magnified many times over.

For a karateist, then, the greater the stress, the better the performance. Sun Tzu, the legendary fifth century B.C. Chinese general, whose essays on war are world-famous, based his philosophy of warfare on the same principles karate is based on. He's said to have forced his troops to fight with their backs to the water whenever possible. He knew this additional stress would encourage his men to fight with more determination. He understood that fear can be a powerful motivator, given the right circumstances.

Just as you must be able to deal with your fear and put it to good use in order to protect yourself, so must you be able to adapt to the particular situation and environment you find yourself in. Karate teaches you how to be more flexible and creative if you're caught off guard.

Fast, flexible, imaginative adaptability is especially important during an attack, when the attacker has the advantage of surprise. As one recently mugged, newly enrolled karate student told me, "He moved in on me before I saw him, knocked me down before I realized he wasn't there to ask me if I had a match, took my ring and my wallet and ran off. It was over before I knew what was happening. What would I have done if he was out to kill me? I'd never have known what the hell was going on—until it was way too late."

In a surprise assault, a karateist can usually react very quickly and effectively. He's been trained to immediately and accurately assess a situation. In addition, he's learned to quickly see what part of his surroundings he can use to help himself.

A karateist can think creatively, especially under pressure.

To the average person, untrained in karate, an old newspaper is litter, something to step over or walk around. To the karateist, it can become a weapon when rolled up tightly, as effective as a billy club. A pencil or a comb can be used as a weapon, in knifelike fashion. A briefcase or pocketbook isn't just a container for papers and possessions. You can use it either as a shield or a club.

Contrary to what most people believe, karate has been, at different stages of its development, as much a weapon-using art as a weaponless one. The karateist is certainly capable of fighting with his bare hands, but he is also adaptable enough to use whatever his surroundings offer him when he needs a weapon.

In the beginning, karate was used by weaponless monks for self-protection. Later, it was practiced by agricultural peasants, who used their farm tools as makeshift weapons. Karate also became the sophisticated fighting art of the ancient Chinese warlords, who developed highly specialized and efficient weapons.

Karate has changed dozens of times to fit the requirements of the people using it. Adaptability has kept karate alive as a means of self-defense—in whatever form—for many centuries. If a fighter's body were the only weapon, he used it. If his physical surroundings could be used, then branches, stones, even water became his arsenal.

Karate is flexible enough to meet the demands of nearly any situation, and the successful karateist of today, like those before him, takes full advantage of this flexibility. How to adapt his art to the environment and his need is something every karate student should learn.

While it can be useful to make a weapon out of something you see lying around, few karateists feel the need to carry a knife or a gun. In karate you have the best weapon with you at all times—your body. You can make weapons of your knuckles, fingers, the ball of your foot, your heel or instep. In karate your arms, legs, hips, back—even your head—become weapons.

As a karateist, you will have at your command a variety of moves specifically designed to use and develop your own unique physical characteristics. Even characteristics that at first glance seem more like hindrances than useful tools can become effective, lifesaving weapons.

Heavy people, for instance, usually think of their weight as a disadvantage. Often, it is. If you are heavy and you're attacked, your weight will slow you down and tire you out in no time. But with training, you'll know how to use your weight as a weapon, making it work for you instead of against you, maneuvering your weight to overwhelm your attacker.

Actually, karate helps you become a specialist—both in adapting the art to fit your own needs and abilities and in adapting yourself to your environment and your situation. For self-defense, this adaptability is crucial, since you'll be dealing with a real-life situation in which there are no rules except the survival of the fittest.

America's two native fighting arts—boxing and street fighting—don't teach you how to deal with fear in the way karate does. Neither are they as versatile nor as adaptable.

The Fighter vs. the Karateist

Ever since its earliest days, boxing has been known as "the manly art of self-defense." But boxing is much more a spectator sport than a method of self-defense. As a fighting art, boxing is far too polite to offer sufficient protection. In the phrase "manly art of self-defense," the word "manly" really means "gentlemanly." Nobility is fine in the ring. But on the streets, in real life, it's dangerous.

The rules of boxing are clear-cut and very limiting. For example, a boxer can't "punch below the belt." In the boxing code this is "fighting dirty." So is hitting one's opponent when he's down. So is using one's feet to kick. A boxer can use only his hands and arms as weapons, and he can aim them only at certain areas of his opponent's body. All these regulations are fine if you're a professional boxer—but they're useless to the average man or woman interested in self-defense.

Karate, unlike boxing, was developed for survival, not sport. The limitations of boxing simply don't exist in karate. A karateist has his feet, head, back, stomach, knees, elbows, *and* hands to rely on. In addition, the karateist knows that no part of his opponent's body is "below the belt." He can hit or kick wherever will do the most damage.

A karateist's strike can travel in any direction, too. Since karate is a multidirectional fighting art, a karateist can handle several attackers simultaneously. His arms and legs, even his head, can move laterally or to the rear, just as easily as they can move to the front. The boxer is limited by his unidirectional art. That is, he must face his opponent at all times and direct his blows forward.

The karate influence is being reflected in American fighting. TV and movie heroes, for example, have become more concerned with surviving against high odds than they are with upholding a clean-cut, all-American image. The gentlemanly code of boxing is being broken here, and that brings us to America's other fighting art—street fighting.

As a means of self-defense, street fighting has a few obvious advantages. It is not limited by styles or rules. Anything goes: knees in the groin, elbows in the ribs, fingers in the eyes. No street fighter ever worries about being a gentleman. There's no such thing as "fighting dirty" in a street fighter's vocabulary.

Why, then, is karate superior to street fighting in a self-defense situation? The karateist can do everything that the street fighter can do, and more. Only better.

The street fighter can count on only two things to save his life during an attack: his strength and his street savvy. Neither of these is particularly reliable when compared to the unlimited resources of the karateist.

Let's talk about strength first. Being powerful and big won't necessarily protect the street fighter during an assault. There's always the possibility that the attacker will be stronger, bigger, and more powerful. On the other hand, the karateist—even one who is small and not particularly strong by conventional standards—can handle an attacker of any size and strength, for he can turn the attacker's power against him. While the street fighter often has to beat his enemy by sheer physical force, the karateist makes his enemy defeat himself.

Street savvy is a combination of fighting experience, familiarity with the situation and instinct. While experience is valuable, it is always limited. Even the street fighter with a great deal of experience may not know how to apply it to a new situation.

The karateist doesn't have to rely on experience or instinct during an attack. His training and his discipline usually give him the upper hand in any threatening situation—the more unfamiliar, the better. With his ability to improvise on the spot, he is far more adaptable

—and far safer—than the street fighter. The karateist knows how to fight for his life with his mind as well as his body. The undisciplined and unsystematic street fighter lacks the advantages of karate logic, karate control, karate thought, karate supercharging, karate's ability to turn fear into an asset.

When You Have No Choice

A karateist fights only when he has to, gets his energy from his fear and his power and control from his mind/body unity, and will use whatever he needs from his environment. But how does he fight? In what way does he defend himself?

Even when he's in battle, the karateist applies the principle of nonconfrontation as much as possible. The notion of dynamic balance, the idea of harmonizing with force, and the concept of the hard and the soft play as important a role in karate combat as they do in the overall philosophy.

In combat the karateist doesn't meet force with more force, but follows the path of least resistance whenever possible. Imagine that a boulder begins rolling down a hill, straight at you. What do you do? Well, you can stand directly in front of it if you want to. You can hold out your hands and try to stop it. If it's a really large boulder, it might roll you flat despite your best efforts to stop it.

Your other choice is not to confront or resist that boulder at all. You can just step lightly to the side—surely the path of least resistance—and let it roll right on past you, carried by its own momentum. If you think it would be useful to you to alter the boulder's course, you can shove it in another direction as it rolls by. Or it might be to your advantage to push the boulder as it passes you, if you want it to roll a little farther than it would on its own.

You can use these same ideas if you're attacked. Imagine that someone is coming at you with all his might. This is the best kind of attack for a karateist to deal with. You're going to rely on your attacker's force and energy. So the harder the attack, the more easily you can defend yourself.

As the attacker lunges at you, you can step aside, just as you would avoid the rolling boulder. This is following the path of least resistance. It's the soft response. And it will surprise your attacker, who is expecting resistance. At that moment your attacker is most vulnerable to any karate technique you may choose.

Deception is one of the keys to karate self-defense. Not only is the soft technique or path of least resistance deceptive, but the individual moves in karate are also deceptive. When you learn karate, you'll begin to see how you can disguise your intentions. A move may start out looking like it's going to be a block, but it might end up being a kick.

In addition to being deceptive, the soft response has another advantage. Because you don't offer resistance—which would stop your attacker's move—he must take a longer time to complete his action. Remember, people are most precariously balanced when they're in motion. The longer you can force your opponent to stay in motion, the more vulnerable he is to your counterattack.

Your attacker's weakness begins the instant he begins his move. That's why, as a karateist, you wait for your opponent to move first. Once the attacker commits himself to a move, he can't turn back. He is vulnerable—and the advantage is yours.

Karate moves are very concise and fast. There's generally no follow-through to prolong the time it takes you to complete a move. Since the moves are brief, a karateist isn't vulnerable (in motion) for a long time. His move ends on impact, and retreat is immediate.

Furthermore, a balanced karate stance gives you a secure base from which to move. You are less vulnerable even while moving than your attacker is. You can remain in a state of dynamic balance during combat. It's a very great advantage.

Patience is a very important part of karate self-defense. If you commit yourself first, you lose some of karate's advantages. You limit your ability to protect your body, to move quickly, to avoid blows, to change your strategy, to deceive your attacker, and to maintain your balance.

There's another karate self-defense rule you should also know: *let your attacker escape if he tries.* If he chooses to run away instead of continue his assault, let him. Your goal is to end the incident as quickly as possible and cause as little pain as possible.

The Shaolin Temple Boxers, the earliest martial artists, lived according to very strict rules of nonviolence. They were not allowed to accept challenges and were not permitted to behave aggressively. There have been many changes in karate through the ages, and no doubt there will be more to come, but I hope and believe the tradition of nonviolence will not be violated. It is such an integral part of the art that without it, karate is no longer karate.

The ancient warlord Sun Tzu didn't interfere with his

enemies' retreat. He allowed them an escape route if he could. He didn't want his opponents to be forced to fight to their deaths—with their backs to the wall. He knew that a man who thinks he is truly cornered and has nothing to lose fights twice as fiercely as before.

It's important to remember, in a self-defense situation, that a desperate man is a far more dangerous opponent than one who thinks he can flee. If you chase an attacker who's trying to escape—or force a fight to continue after your attacker's given up—you're creating an unnecessary risk for both of you.

Most people fear an attacker without a weapon almost as much as they fear one who is armed. But I hardly need say that if you're attacked by a gunman, you're in more danger than if your attacker has no weapon. Even a knife isn't as dangerous as a gun. In order to stab you with a knife, an attacker has to commit himself to a move. As I've mentioned, this gives a karateist at least a momentary advantage.

But no karateist, however skilled, is a match for a bullet. Karate was developed before the advent of handguns and was not designed to deal with them. In fact, had handguns existed in ancient days, it's an open question as to whether or not the martial arts would ever have been developed to their present extent.

When confronted by a gunman (or even a man with a knife), the karateist must do everything in his power to keep the encounter nonviolent. If necessary, he or she must submit to the attacker's demands. However, if the karateist's life is in *imminent* danger, or if serious—possibly fatal—injury is about to take place, anything goes. This is the time for the karateist to use all his skills—and anything else he can think of.

Chapter 9
Other Places, Other Times

In my view, the development of karate is one of mankind's most remarkable achievements. As a way of fulfilling human abilities and filling human needs, it deserves to be ranked with the invention of writing and the development of mathematics. Yet we will never be able to honor any one man for initiating this achievement. Even Bodhidharma, extraordinary though he must have been, only united two preexisting martial arts forms—those of China and India. Eventually, no doubt, they would have merged without him.

Prehistoric Karate

The true origins of karate stretch back into the mists of time. The martial arts as we know them today are but highly refined expressions of some very basic human instincts. It would surprise me if the cavemen hadn't practiced some crude form of open-handed or closed-fist self-defense or fighting.

In fact, a good case can be made for the notion that such techniques are not simply the expression of human instincts, but go much deeper into our evolutionary history, reflecting some basic animal instincts. After all, a number of highly developed animals—kangaroos, bears, big cats, monkeys, apes, gorillas, etc.—use the "hands" for fighting or self-defense.

What man did was to take these elemental drives and subject them to his intelligence. He added a philosophy and a rationale to them. He made them into a system that mirrored his own development and served his needs —and not just his self-defense needs, as we have seen, but also his mental and emotional needs. Even now, the forms of karate—the *katas*—are formalized combat movements. Though learning them leads to a host of benefits that have nothing to do with violence, they are intrinsically violent.

You may wonder why you should learn a basically militant art (aside from reasons of self-defense) in this day and age. Though we live in a violent period of history, we rightly deplore violence, since it is the cruelest of human actions. Won't the widespread learning and practice of karate create more violence?

I think not. The way I see it, the need to experience violence—to express aggression and hostility—is a basic human drive. It cannot be eliminated merely through abstention and thinking peaceful thoughts. It must somehow be discharged.

Humanity has invented a wide variety of ways to discharge its innate violent impulses—sports, games, competitions, and the like. But, obviously, these substitutes haven't been enough. Humanity has chosen to express its aggressive drives both individually and collectively, one person toward another, one nation toward another.

To my mind, the *katas* are the ideal way to discharge the human need to experience and express violence. They are, at their core, combative. And yet, in effect, when practiced in any way but for self-defense, they are nonviolent. They offer an outlet for hostile aggression, an equivalent of war, but without injurious effect.

To be sure, there are people—many people—who bottle up their hostilities and aggressive drives. Trouble is, in the end these instincts can't be bottled up. Strong evidence from many sources suggests that when people have no external outlet for their aggressions, they turn on themselves. To one degree or another, they become self-destructive, even suicidal.

Quite aside from all its personal benefits, then, karate offers a profound social benefit. By providing an outlet for human aggressive drives, by offering a way to discharge violent impulses, karate can serve as a lightning rod for actual violence.

I strongly believe that when the knowledge and practice of karate becomes widespread in the United States—and I feel it will—the result will be a less violent society, not a more violent one. Anger, aggression, and hostility will be discharged and used up in the practice of the *katas*, not on the streets. There is even reason to believe that, should karate become universal, the chances of war would be reduced. After all, what is war if not the extension of composite individual need?

The theory I'm propounding isn't original with me,

of course. Similar notions have been advanced by such ethnologists as Konrad Lorenz and Robert Ardrey. Lorenz, for example, has labeled aggressive drives "a hereditary evil of mankind," the product of "roughly 40,000 years of struggling against starvation, freezing, being eaten by wild animals, and fending off hostile neighbors. Lorenz has called for an investigation of all the possibilities of discharging aggression via "substitute forms"—that is, not against other people. He feels this "ritualization of aggression" is both practical and necessary.

Looking at war, Robert Ardrey has pointed out that "it has been the all-purpose answer to our innate needs. Now, advancing technology may force us to abandon [it]. But, we cannot discard from human expression an institution so outrageously satisfying without discovering and encouraging substitute outlets."

To my mind, karate and the other martial arts are the perfect substitute. Not only do they burn off our aggressive drives, but they also help us reach our full potential in almost every other area of life.

Origins and Development

The martial arts that dominate the world today were mainly developed in the Orient. But similar arts sprang up in ancient times all over the world, as mankind evolved first in little, isolated communities, then in civilizations.

Actually, the oldest definite records of unarmed combat come not from the Orient but from the Middle East. They can be seen in the pyramids today—hieroglyphics dating back to 4000 B.C. describing boxinglike fighting techniques used by ancient Egyptian warriors. Similar records dating back to 3000 B.C. have been found in the ruins of Sumer, in what was once a land known as Mesopotamia and is now part of southern Iraq, and in the remains of Bein Hasan in Egypt (about 2300 B.C.).

Karatelike combat also turns up in Western records. The Greek poet Homer, who is believed to have lived around 800–900 B.C., described fights of this sort in the 23rd book of the *Iliad*.

Unarmed combat, usually in the form of boxing matches, became a fixture of long-ago Greek society. Theogenes, a champion Greek boxer of the fifth century, B.C., is said to have knocked out 2,102 opponents, killing about 1,800.

The Greek philosopher Plato, who lived between 427 and 347 B.C., wrote about *skiamachia* ("fighting without an opponent"), a kind of shadow boxing. And in his day there were military "dances" called *pyrrhichia* ("how to cope with an enemy"). These, of course, are counterparts of the *kata*.

We know that these techniques were used in combat from the story of Creugas and Damoxenus, two Greek fighters of Plato's day. Sometime around the year 400 B.C., they met in a match at Nemea. According to historical records, they fought from dawn to dusk without deciding the match. Finally, they decided to give each other one final blow—unopposed—to determine the winner.

Creugas hit Damoxenus in the head with all his might, but Damoxenus survived the blow. Then he ordered Creugas to raise his left arm. Creugas obeyed. Damoxenus then struck Creugas a spearlike blow with his open hand, driving his extended fingers into his opponent's side, killing him. Statues of the two fighters, in their final postures before that last blow, can be seen today in the Vatican.

Eventually the Greeks combined what they called wrestling with their form of boxing, into something called the *pancratium,* a fighting system in which the entire body was used as a weapon and in which there was no such thing as a foul. The Greeks abandoned this method of fighting, but the Romans revived it for gladitorial combat. The Roman gladiators, of course, were the Western equivalent of Oriental karateists—though, since Taoism and Buddhism were essentially unknown in the West, the emphasis was almost entirely on combat.

By the way, even in those days, Greek and Roman fighters weren't above demonstrating their physical prowess by breaking stones and rocks with their bare hands while spectators watched.

There is also some evidence that karatelike techniques developed in areas far from the main thrust of both Eastern and Western civilization. A number of different authorities have found traces of unarmed combat systems among the ancient Incas, among the Celts in prehistoric Britain, among the Vikings, and among certain American Indian tribes.

But it was only in the Orient—mainly China—where these forms of combat continued to develop, evolving not only in the physical sense, but also in the philosophical sense.

Not long after Bodhidharma taught the Shaolin Temple monks "the Eighteen Hands of the Lo-Han"—the physical drills that were the basis for *kung fu*—he died. Eventually his disciples dispersed and the art was nearly lost. Many years later—some authorities say decades, some say centuries—a man named Ch'ueh Yuan recast Bodhidharma's eighteen movements and added many of his own, bringing the number up to seventy-two. As legend has it, he still did not feel he'd perfected the art, so he went in search of other masters.

One day, he saw an old peddler being attacked by a bully. While Ch'ueh Yuan watched, the bully—we'd call him a mugger today—lashed out with a savage kick. The old man merely touched the bully's foot with his fingers, and his larger, stronger opponent fell to the ground, unconscious.

It was through this peddler that Ch'ueh Yuan met Pai Yu-feng, the local master, a kindly, spiritual man in his fifties. Together they returned to the Shaolin Temple in northern China, where they further expanded *kung fu,* to about 170 different hand and foot positions.

To these physical movements, Ch'ueh Yuan added some moral precepts. The most important: The art should be used only for legitimate self-defense; a student must be forever kind, honest, and friendly to all his colleagues; a "boxer" must never be bellicose; "boxing" should not be taught rashly to non-Buddhists, lest it produce harm. It can only be transmitted to one who is gentle and merciful.

According to legend, students could not graduate from the Shaolin temple until they passed three tests, and they had to pass the first two before they could undertake the third. The tests were:

1. A thorough oral examination on the history and theory of the art

2. Combat with several of the most accomplished monks

3. A life-or-death trip through a sealed labyrinth whose single exit was the temple's front gate.

The labyrinth is said to have contained 108 mechanized dummies with wooden fists, spears, knives, and other weapons. These dummies were apparently triggered by boards on the labyrinth's floor, so that the student himself caused them to attack him.

If the student survived the dummies and got to the front gate, he still could not leave until he was able to pick up and move a 500-lb. urn full of boiling oil. To lift it, the student had to wrap his arms around the urn, his forearms pressed firmly against symbols of a dragon on one side and a tiger on the other, burning their images into his skin forever. The only way a student could lift this urn—which was too heavy for even the strongest man, under normal conditions—was to unite and focus his total *chi* on the task.

For five hundred years or so after Bodhidharma's death, *kung fu* developed according to the principles laid down by that master, by Ch'ueh Yuan, and by Pai Yu-feng. But there were literally hundreds of offshoots and variations on the original forms and styles, each one with its own masters and schools. Many of these emphasized or borrowed from animal movements—the Eagle Claw system, the Praying Mantis system, the White Crane system, and so on.

Somewhere between A.D. 960 and 1268, during the Sung dynasty, while Britain was being invaded by the Normans and the Magna Carta was being signed, a

Taoist monk, who was also an ardent follower of Confucius and the *I Ching*, took a closer look at Shaolin Temple boxing and its offshoots. His name was Chang San-feng.

Apparently disheartened by the hard, offensive, and mostly external characteristics of Shaolin Temple boxing, Chang San-feng decided to create a new system, one that would emphasize the soft, the internal, and the defensive.

According to legend, his inspiration came one day during his noon meditation. He heard a strange noise in the courtyard and looked out the window. He saw a snake, its head raised, hissing at a crane sitting in a tree above it. The crane flew down and attacked the snake with its spearlike beak, but the snake turned its head aside and attacked the crane's neck with its tail.

The crane used its right wing to shield its neck, but the snake shifted its attack to the crane's legs. The crane raised its left leg and lowered its left wing to beat off the snake, while stabbing at it with its beak. But it couldn't land a solid blow. The snake always managed to twist or bend out of reach.

Finally, bored or exhausted, the crane flew back to a high branch in the tree, and the snake slithered back into its hole. The next day, the entire episode repeated itself, and the next—always with Chang San-feng watching. Eventually, he began to realize that he was seeing a demonstration of the value of yielding in the face of strength in order to become strong.

After studying the crane, the snake, and other animals and natural elements, Chang San-feng codified what he'd learned into a system of movements, many of which had animal names, such as White Crane Spreads Wings and Snake Creeps Down. From his system eventually came *tai chi ch'uan* ("grand ultimate fist") and its sister arts, all slow, graceful and enormously complex and difficult to master, all strongly influenced by Taoism.

It doesn't matter much whether or not the crane-and-snake legend is true, though it would be nice to think it was. What matters is that the Shaolin, or "hard" methods now had some competition. Ironically, the soft methods also originated with Bodhidharma, since his original eighteen movements, so far as is known, were basically "soft."

In the centuries that followed, both systems and their many variations flourished. They were kept vital by China's many secret societies, groups that fought political oppression and rebelled against autocracy. When the infamous Manchus swept out of Manchuria and took control of China in 1644, the secret societies spread their combat skills throughout the land, hoping to throw out the invaders. But they failed.

Eventually, other foreign invaders came to China's shores—among them the British, French, Germans, Portuguese. These Western nations came to dominate China, and they became objects of great hatred.

In 1900 the secret societies staged the famous Boxer Rebellion—the word "boxer" referring to many systems of *kung fu,* out of which karate eventually came. Actually, there was very little fighting of the *kung fu* variety, though both the Chinese rulers and the peasantry seem to have been hypnotized by the martial artists into thinking they could defeat Western arms without weapons. Most fighting on both sides, however, was done with weapons.

There was an unsuccessful attempt to make *kung fu* into a national sport during the 1920s and 1930s, an attempt ended by World War II. After the war, when the communists rose to power, many practitioners of the martial arts retreated south to Taiwan with Chiang Kai-shek, or they went to Hong Kong, Singapore, Indochina, and the United States.

Today, the martial arts continue to flourish in Communist China, as part of Mao Tse-tung's gymnastic and self-defense programs. Magazines and newspapers emphasize their value, both for personal self-improvement and as a national resource and tradition.

Karate Here and There

Meanwhile, many other Asian nations developed martial art forms of their own, usually variations on the Chinese model, or combinations of Chinese and Indian influence, often with native elements thrown in. Again, there are hundreds of systems, in dozens of countries, most of which you've probably never heard of and never will, since they aren't important outside their countries of origin.

But a few systems have come to have a major impact on the teaching and study of the martial arts. They're worth describing briefly so that you'll have a general idea of what they are, should you read about them or hear them discussed.

Let's take them on a country-by-country basis:

Korea. The original empty-handed fighting method in Korea was known as *t'ang-su* ("Tang hand"), whose very name refers to its origins in the Tang dynasty of China (A.D. 618–907). Over the centuries, this art gave birth to several variations: *kwonpup, tae kwon,* and others, which rose and fell in popularity with Korean military conditions.

When Korea became independent from China in 1945, these arts were modernized into *tae kwon do*, which bears great similarities to its Chinese ancestors and to other modern Asian martial arts.

While *tae kwon do* involves punching, jumping kicks, blocks, dodges, parrying actions with hands and feet, and the like, it is also a way of thinking and a pattern of life, as is karate. And it also emphasizes correct breathing, unifying the *chi*, and so on.

Indonesia. The national form of unarmed combat in this country is known mainly as *pentjak-silat*, a term defined as "fighting by means of regulated, skillful body movements in variations and combinations."

Legend has it—there's always a legend—that the art began with the observations of a peasant woman. Long ago, on Indonesia's northernmost island—Sumatra—a woman went to get some water in a stream and ended up watching a tiger fight a large bird. After several hours, both combatants died.

After half the day had passed, the woman's husband came looking for her, angry at her absence. He lashed out to hit her again and again, but she easily evaded his blows by imitating the dodges of the animals she'd been watching.

Later, she taught her skills to her chastened husband, and *pentjak-silat* was born. The truth is, *pentjak-silat* probably got its animal inspirations from the Hindu culture of relatively nearby India. And many of the art's variations have animal names: "ape style," "bat style," "tiger style," "snake style," and the like. Chinese influence, what there is of it, probably dates from more recent times.

Pentjak-silat, when seen in public, looks like a carefully controlled exercise. Its basic forms resemble *katas,* though they're less formal and more fluid. Some forms include weapons.

Very often, a form of the art is performed at festivals and weddings, in a competitive way, sometimes accompanied by music. This has given some observers the false impression that it is a dance.

The combat forms of the art are secret and never shown in public. They're said to use hypnosis or strong suggestion, both of one's opponent and of oneself (in order to achieve a trancelike state). Little is known about these forms, at least to non-Indonesians.

Masters of *pentjak-silat* are regarded first as spiritualists —followers of a philosophy—and second as practitioners of the physical art.

Malaya. Malaya is even closer to India than is Indonesia, and it is likely that Indian influence on its methods of unarmed combat are correspondingly greater. The name of the national martial art is *bersilat* ("to do fighting") and it has much in common with *pentjak-silat*—as far as we know, since its techniques are generally kept secret.

It exists in two forms today—*silat pulat,* for public display, and *silat buah,* for combat. The second of these forms is practiced alone, taught in secret and under a vow of silence.

In both Malaya and Indonesia, an eclectic Chinese martial art, *kun-tao* or *kun-tow,* is also popular. It's a blend of the external and internal systems, and resembles certain Chinese forms.

Thailand. There are all kinds of unarmed combat systems in this country, but the most famous is known as "Thai boxing." It looks very much like Western boxing—

roped fighting ring, gloves, trunks, and so forth. But it includes quick, high kicks to the opponent's head or chest.

The art is thought to date back to about 1560, when King Naresuen of Siam was captured by the Burmese and given the opportunity for freedom if he could defeat the Burmese champ. He did—and gave his country a sport.

And sport is exactly what "Thai boxing" is, in much the same way Western boxing is a sport. There are hundreds of professional boxers in the country and hundreds of training camps. It's as popular as baseball or basketball is in America.

Burma. Since it lies directly between India and China, it's not surprising that Burma's fighting arts have been influenced by both countries, though India's influence came first.

The national martial art is known as *bando,* and it closely resembles other Asian martial arts, both in the way it is taught and in appearance. The way it was taught by the Buddhist monks in the past stressed breathing and meditation techniques and yielding, or nonconfrontation ideas.

Most *bando* schools today teach footholds and basic postures, then blocking and parrying forms, and finally, offensive techniques. These are based on animal motions. The boar form, for example, emphasizes courage, rushing, elbowing, kneeing, and butting. The tiger form stresses clawing and ripping.

The Philippines. The best-known martial art in this nation is known as *arnis de mano* ("harness of hands"), a term taken from a Spanish expression. The art employs one or two hardwood sticks about thirty inches long and an inch thick. Hand and stick movements are more important than body movements.

Today most Filipinos regard *arnis* as either a form of self-defense or as a sport. In fact, since 1949, the provinces have held annual tournaments in the art.

Many other Asian countries have their own martial arts—Mongolia, Vietnam, Taiwan, Cambodia, India, etc. But for our purposes, they are either derivative (usually from some Chinese form) or no longer widely practiced or popular. There are two exceptions to this—countries whose contributions to the martial arts almost rival China's: Okinawa and Japan. They deserve our close consideration, for they made karate what it is today.

Okinawa. This is the main island of the Ryukyu island chain, which stretches from Japan, in the north, almost to China, in the south. Racially, it appears to be a mixture of Japanese and Southeast Asian stock.

Long before the Chinese set foot on Okinawa—though history is vague here—the islanders apparently developed their own form of unarmed combat, something called *tode* (pronounced toe-day). This is reflected in age-old classical dances, in which the part danced by the men closely resembles modern karate movements.

Historians argue about when the Chinese forms of the martial arts came to Okinawa. Some think the island was exposed to these influences as early as A.D. 600. Others believe it was not until 1300 or so. No records on the subject, either written or oral, seem to exist on Okinawa itself.

During Europe's medieval period, Okinawa was a crossroads island, a natural stopping-off place for Japanese diplomats on the way to China and vice versa. Its natives were active traders and diplomats themselves. As a result, Okinawa tasted of many Asian cultures, incorporating many foreign ideas into its own way of living. This was particularly true of the martial arts.

During this period, forms and concepts from Vietnam, Thailand, Indonesia, and other countries were added to the preexisting Japanese-Chinese mixture.

It was Okinawa's unique history that made it the birthplace of karate, rather than the genius of any one man. In 1372 the Okinawan king swore allegiance to China. But the Japanese dominated the island, except when Chinese tax collectors stopped by.

So it went for more than two hundred years. Then, in 1600, two decades before the pilgrims landed at Plymouth Rock, there was a civil war in Japan. As was customary in that country, the winning side—the great Tokugawa clan—gave the losing side—the almost as great Satsuma clan—a consolation prize. That prize turned out to be Okinawa and the other Ryukyu islands.

Not surprisingly, the Satsumas did not turn out to be benevolent rulers of their new territory. On the contrary —they were oppressive and vindictive. And they issued one small edict that changed the course of martial arts history: they ordered the Okinawans to give up all their weapons—even, eventually, their ceremonial swords. They wanted to be sure their new vassals had no means of resistance.

But the Okinawans were a proud people, not about to submit to total subjugation. They fought again and again, with the only weapons they had: their bare hands and feet.

During this period, the Okinawans blended their native *tode* system of unarmed combat with Chinese *kung fu* techniques and with what they'd picked up from other cultures. They came up with an art they called *te*, "hand," which closely resembles modern karate. (The word *te* can also mean "power-fraught," a power which comes from fear.)

Te was taught underground, to avoid discovery by the Satsumas, in conditions of extreme secrecy. And it was used by secret societies against their Japanese oppressors, both in ambush and in pitched battle.

Although the Okinawans had no weapons, the developers of *te* cleverly made weapons out of everyday tools and farm implements: the *bo*, a nearly six-foot staff; the *kama*, a sickle; the *tui-fa*, a millstone handle; and the *nunchaku*, a wooden flail.

In 1875 the Satsuma occupation of Okinawa officially ended. Okinawa and the other Ryukyu islands became part of Japan, beginning a process of assimilation that was not really complete until the beginning of World War II.

In 1903 the art—now called karate—became a regular part of the physical education curriculum in the Okinawan schools, a position it holds today.

Japan. The Japanese of the late nineteenth century were very impressed with karate, though they knew little about it, since the Okinawans tried to keep their art as secret as possible. But, while World War I was taking place on the other side of the globe, Crown Prince Hirohito saw a karate exhibition on Okinawa and decided this was an art the Japanese army should know.

Of course, Japan already had its own martial arts forms—many of them. Even in its ancient days, unarmed combat in many forms was an essential part of the culture. References to what appear to be karatelike combat between various mythological gods are common in early Japanese literature, and many authorities believe these were inspired by actual struggles.

Just how these arts came to Japan—what part was native, what part was Chinese, when and how they were mixed—is a matter of great debate among historians.

But eventually several dozen different fighting arts developed, some involving bow-and-arrow forms, some basically horsemanship or swordsmanship, some using various weapons.

For our purposes, the most important techniques are the empty-hand systems of combat, of which there are several broad categories:

- *Sumo*, or Japanese wrestling, now mainly a sport but once a deadly combat art that included kicking, butting and striking.
- *Jujutsu* (usually misspelled *juijitsu* or *jujitsu* in the United States), a general term for fighting systems that stress unarmed combat but also teach the use of small weapons. Jujutsu mainly emphasizes throwing the opponent and learning how to fall yourself— the principles of modern judo, which is a competitive sport rather than a system of self-defense. The key tactic in this art is to pretend to yield to an opponent, then use his own motion to throw him or otherwise beat him.

  In all, there are more than seven hundred jujutsu systems in Japan.
- *Aikido*. This martial art is a relatively modern development, the brainchild of one M. Ueshiba, who began to devise it in the early 1900s, after studying more than two hundred other martial arts forms. What Ueshiba was looking for was something that would allow him to develop his own spirituality and body. By 1942 he'd finished perfecting his system, which draws heavily on traditional forms.

  Today *aikido* is a way of life encompassing the concepts of *chi* and the philosophy of the *Tao*. It also stresses inner values, a harmonious unification of mind and body.

In its fighting form, *aikido* is a defensive technique meant to ward off attacks or throw opponents to the ground. Wristlocks, armlocks, and throws characterize the art.

What place does Okinawan karate have among all these forms of unarmed combat?

Let's go back a bit, to 1922. In that year the Japanese Ministry of Education invited Gichin Funakoshi, one of Okinawa's greatest karateists, to give a demonstration in Tokyo. Funakoshi, to prove that the Okinawans were finally beginning to forgive and forget, consented.

Funakoshi stayed on in Japan, demonstrating karate at universities all over the country. Eventually, he was joined by other famous Okinawan karate masters and the art spread throughout Japan. By 1932, nearly all Japanese universities had their own *dojos*—karate schools.

At this time, karate—for that matter, most of the Asian forms of unarmed combat—were mostly unknown in the West. But something was about to occur that would change all that: World War II.

Chapter 10
Karate for the Western World

For reasons that are lost to history, the martial arts never developed in the West the way they did in the Orient. Maybe this was because the Europeans were accomplished technologists. They had the scientific knowledge necessary to perfect projectile weapons: bows and arrows, cannons, rifles, and handguns. These weapons made it unnecessary to develop hand-to-hand combat techniques, at least to the state of perfection they attained in Okinawa, where all weapons were banned.

At any rate, while karate was flourishing throughout the Far East, the Europeans were busy exploring the world, planting colonies in faraway places, and settling new lands. Aside from street brawling and boxing, they did their fighting aboard magnificent floating men-of-war, or in huge massed armies armed with muskets and backed by artillery.

If the settlers of the New World had been interested in karatelike forms, or felt the need of them, they might have adopted a system of unarmed combat native to the Americas. There is firm evidence that the Indians developed a karatelike martial art of their own, based on breathing techniques and animal forms. From what I understand, these fighting arts survive even today and are practiced by certain Indian tribes that live on Western reservations.

Instead, European settlers chose to defend themselves with the superior weaponry of their technology; and, in the end, Indians ended up adopting rifles rather than colonists learning Indian fighting arts.

Oddly enough, the Americans had a chance to see and take up yet another civilization's martial arts system: that of the slaves imported from Africa. African tribes, like primitive people in other parts of the world, had invented their own method of hand-to-hand combat— strikingly like karate, though not as highly developed.

This martial art was frequently practiced in the southern United States in the slave era, often during escape attempts. But as far as I know, it has entirely died out in this country, though it continues to exist in various forms in its homeland.

I don't know if any of our forefathers saw or heard of the martial arts as they were practiced in the Orient, during the first 150 years of this country's existence. Frankly, I doubt it. Western commerce with the Orient in those days was limited. In fact, until the British defeated China in the Opium War of 1839–42, China had restricted Western merchants to a single port. The

Chinese government did not want to import foreign
ideas or foreign goods (especially British opium grown
in India), and it wasn't much interested in sharing any
of China's best ideas with the West.

After 1842, China reluctantly opened several ports to
European and American ships. But our fast clippers
brought back tea and silk and rice—not martial arts
systems.

Japan was even more closed to the West than China.
Until 1853, it too limited Western ships to a single port:
Nagasaki. But on July 8 of that year, Commodore
Matthew C. Perry sailed a four-ship American fleet into
Tokyo and overawed the shaky Japanese government. As
a result, the Japanese opened two more ports to the
Americans and allowed a substantial expansion of trade.
But Perry and the trading ships that followed brought
back no word of karate. The Japanese kept that to
themselves.

Strange as it seems, Americans brushed close to the
Oriental martial arts twice more during those early
years—but on American soil, not Chinese or Japanese.

The first of these occasions came as a result of the
great California gold strike of 1848. When word of this
find spread across the world, prospectors of every conceivable nationality were attracted to our West Coast.
Between 1848 and 1852, the population of California
swelled from 20,000 to 223,000. Among the newcomers
were 25,000 Chinese, hoping, like everyone else, to strike
it rich.

Almost certainly, there were martial arts practitioners
in this group. But instead of becoming integrated into
American society, the Chinese occupied small enclaves—
Chinatowns. They neither absorbed our ideas nor taught
us theirs.

A decade later, America had another opportunity to learn about *kung fu* from the Chinese. Beginning in 1863, Charles Crocker, an executive of the Central Pacific Railroad, began hiring the Chinese that had come during the Gold Rush to work on the railroad. Some railroad men had reservations about the strength of the 110-lb. coolies, but they soon proved able to work alongside the burliest Irish laborers. By the middle 1860s, Chinese workers by the thousands were being imported from the farm districts of Canton. And they deserve great credit for the rapid spread of railroads over the face of America.

There can be no doubt that some of these laborers were also practitioners of *kung fu*. But there is no record that they taught the art to any of their Irish colleagues or to any American railroaders.

On the other hand, the historical truth does make the sometimes silly "Kung Fu" television series seem a bit more credible, when you think about it.

Instead of introducing elements of Chinese culture into the United States and spreading Chinese ideas among Americans, the great influx of Chinese laborers during the railroad-building era produced strong anti-Oriental feelings here.

Secrecy and Tradition

Americans had nothing in particular against the Chinese, except that they had strange customs (they drank tea and bathed daily), they looked different, and they were competitors on the job market—a combination usually leading to prejudice. Still, by the end of the nineteenth century many Chinese had decided to call America home. They didn't do much mingling with native-born Americans, however, instead creating self-contained Chinatowns.

Within these communities, Chinese culture flourished. So did bitter conflict between various factions, over which would control gambling, prostitution, and the like. The result were the famous "tong wars" between various secret societies, which didn't completely end until the 1930s.

These "wars"—like struggles between different Mafia factions—were fought by "hatchet men," who used meat cleavers to kill their enemies and who were also skilled at *kung fu* and at the art of pin-blowing (with a human being as a target) and the throwing of razor-sharp coins.

Some Chinese on the way to California never got there at all, instead stopping in Hawaii and settling there. Exclusive Chinese societies—open only to those of Chinese background—were formed there as early as 1889. *Kung fu* clubs—definitely not open to Westerners—sprang up starting in 1922.

On the other hand, non-Chinese did have an opportunity to glimpse *kung fu* practitioners every year during the Chinese New Year celebrations held in February. But the *kung fu* part of these celebrations is usually performed by inexperienced youths, whose inexperience made the art seem haphazard and more acrobatic than martial.

Prejudice against those of Oriental descent stayed at a high level in California. At one point, the friction produced open talk of war on both sides—and remember, this was during *Teddy* Roosevelt's regime, not Franklin's. Teddy Roosevelt found it necessary to transfer the entire American battle fleet from the Atlantic to the Pacific and sent it on a "goodwill cruise" to—among other places—Japan. This show of American determination and strength ended war talk on both sides. But it did nothing to end prejudice in California.

Because of its racial mixture, things went better for the Japanese in Hawaii. And it was there that karate took root. The first documented practitioner of the art arrived there in 1905, the first recognized master in 1927. Though there were a few public demonstrations of the art at that time, most Hawaiian karateists kept their knowledge secret and practiced in the privacy of their homes.

Nothing much happened to improve the American attitude toward Orientals in the years following Teddy Roosevelt's administration. Meanwhile, in Hawaii, karate was becoming quite popular. A number of schools had opened. One karate club, the Hawaii Young People's Karate Club, gave a demonstration at the Honolulu Civic Auditorium, a presentation attended by a number of Caucasians, most of them from the First Methodist Church, which was located near one of the schools.

This obscure demonstration was actually an historic event, so far as Western karate is concerned. As a direct result of it, a number of church members formed the first known Caucasian karate club in 1933. Three Japanese-American instructors taught there.

One of these Western karateists was a member of the U.S. Army Air Corps and coach of Wheeler Air Field's boxing and wrestling teams. His efforts brought some visiting Okinawan karate masters to Wheeler to teach American flyers.

But karate was still an esoteric art insofar as the West

was concerned, and its teaching did not become wide-spread at this time. In fact, it nearly ceased altogether in 1936, when the largest American karate club folded after its founder's retirement.

A Cultural Interchange

The cultural interchange that led to the growth of karate in this country began only after World War II was over; even then it went slowly, despite the fact that thousands of American soldiers did occupation duty in Japan and Okinawa.

There were several reasons Americans didn't take to karate and the Japanese didn't take to teaching it to Westerners immediately following World War II. One was the continued anti-Oriental prejudice on the part of the Americans. Another was the bitter anti-American feelings held by many Japanese after the war.

Eventually, close contact between the races began to soften these mutual feelings of distrust. Nonetheless, Americans did not flock to Japanese karate *dojos*, nor were they invited.

For one thing, *kung fu* and karate masters have always been reluctant to share their art with outsiders—even Oriental outsiders. Historically, in both China and Okinawa, martial arts knowledge has been a military secret of sorts.

Even in ancient days, martial arts knowledge was passed from generation to generation with extreme de-ception and secrecy, so that it would not be learned by outsiders. Years ago, for instance, I found a highly decorated terra cotta vase in an antique store. The decorations seemed to be in a floral pattern. But when I looked closely, I saw the flowers were actually tiny human figures doing various *kata*.

Even the *kata* themselves do not reveal their secrets easily. The untutored observer can watch a karateist go through the *kata* without understanding the meaning and use of each move. And that's no accident.

In the case of *kung fu*, there was an unwritten law against teaching those not of Chinese descent the most important aspects of the art even as recently as the late 1950s. After that, some schools apparently taught Caucasians and Orientals alike—but they taught certain techniques only to Orientals, at a different time and place.

Karate and *kung fu* masters were not even terribly interested in teaching their art to their own countrymen—or at least, not all of their art. The masters kept secrets because that was the traditional way of teaching, because they were following the Zen principle of "never teaching too clearly," because they were afraid a full disclosure would allow their system to be compared with others, because they wanted to feel superior, or simply because they were innately nasty individuals.

As a result, literally thousands of schools and organizations devoted to the martial arts came into being, all at war with the others, each jealously guarding its secrets, each insisting that its system was the best or the purest, each claiming that all others were inferior, or fake, or diluted, or stolen.

The students who graduated—those who got black belts—from these schools found that they owed a homage, a tribute, to their teachers. They could not pass on what they had learned without permission from the master.

And then they had to pay him a kickback for every student they took on.

If the graduate disobeyed and went off on his own and founded a school without permission, he could be disowned by his teacher and his ranking vacated. He'd be defrocked. It was as if the graduate became the permanent property of his teacher, or that the knowledge he learned was always owned by its originator.

This situation prevailed—it still does—throughout the Far East, in China, Japan, Okinawa, Korea, and elsewhere. Similar confusion and dissension exists in the United States and other Western countries in which the martial arts have become popular.

So even if a Westerner wanted to learn karate in the years immediately following World War II, he was in for a rough time of it. In addition, there were some good reasons for not wanting to learn—even for the athletically inclined.

First, Westerners were put off by karate's overload of mystique and Oriental philosophical overtones, not to mention the language difficulties and the odd uniforms. It seemed so, well, un-American and inscrutable. Second, those Westerners who did dabble in karate in those days, usually soldiers in the American army of occupation, usually learned only a smattering of the physical part of the art—and nothing of the philosophy.

The karate they brought home, then, looked brutal and violent. Maybe this was partly because of the personalities of those early Western karateists, many of whom were brawlers to begin with, interested in karate because it would make them more lethal. Also, they simply mimicked without understanding. They did not duplicate.

However, despite the natural deceptiveness of the art,

despite the jealous possessiveness of the masters, despite the mystique and the overtones of brutality, Americans gradually became interested in karate and began to learn it.

It's interesting to consider how this happened. No doubt, the most important factor was the continuing U.S. military presence in Japan and Okinawa. This went on during the occupation of Japan, the Korean war, and the Vietnam war.

During this time, thousands upon thousands of American soldiers and marines lived in close contact with the Japanese, both in Japan proper and on Okinawa, sometimes over a period of several years. As a result of this contact, to some degree, and because of the benevolence of the occupying forces and America's economic aid to Japan, the Japanese more and more began to modify their anti-American attitudes.

Back in the States, Americans were also changing their attitude toward Japan and the Japanese. The country was proving to be a stalwart ally in the Far East, especially important with a China that had turned communist. Also, Japan was an enthusiastic imitator of many Western habits and traditions—copying everything from baseball to miniskirts to the products of our industrial society. And we saw that imitation as the sincerest form of flattery. In addition, the Japanese began to win the admiration of Americans by showing themselves a vigorous, inventive people. The Nikons, Sonys, Toyotas, and Hondas sent here from Japan earned our respect and helped weaken prejudices.

More and more, we became intrigued with all things Japanese, as we had once been intrigued by the products and ideas of European culture.

At the same time, changes within American society

made us more susceptible to karate—even in the fragmented, brutalized form in which it had first become
known to us. With crime and violence on the increase,
many Americans were drawn to karate, either because
they felt it was in tune with their own violent natures or
because it offered a likely defense against the violence
of others.

At about this time the media latched on to karate and
the other martial arts and really began to popularize
them. There were not only tales of board- or brick-
breaking, but also depictions of karate (or something
similar) in the extremely popular James Bond and other
films.

All these changes, together, set the stage for the entry
of the martial arts into American society.

In 1953 the United States Air Force, which had been
interested in Oriental forms of unarmed combat ever
since the occupation of Japan began, brought karate
instructors from three Japanese universities to military
bases in the United States, to teach personnel there.

As far as I know, this was the first time Japanese instructors had taught the martial arts to Westerners on
American soil. Since 1965 there has been a virtual karate
"explosion"—not only in the United States, but also in
Canada, South America, Europe, and even Asia. It was
during this period that the first generation of American
karateists made their appearance on the scene. Most of
these early teachers were either stationed in Okinawa
(or Japan) sometime in the 1950s or learned from marines
or soldiers who were.

Almost as soon as karate began to spread throughout
the U.S., Americans sought to remake it to suit themselves and to put it to typically American uses.

Partly because of the American love of the practical and partly because the early teachers hadn't stayed in the Orient long enough to learn the philosophy behind karate, it was taught here on an *outside-in* basis, rather than an *inside-out* basis. That is, the entire emphasis was on the technology of the art: the *kata* and their many moves. Little, if anything, was said about inner meanings and values—at least at first.

Even now, this emphasis remains. And I think that's the way it should be. Karate has its eminently practical aspects, and there's no reason these can't be taught first. The deeper aspects of the art will practically teach themselves, in time, if the student sticks with it long enough.

Like all cultures that have tried their hand at the martial arts, we have begun to adapt them to our own needs and styles. For instance, we have honored some of karate's Oriental traditions, but dropped others. We retain the traditional uniform, the *gi* (as in geese), because it's an eminently practical and comfortable outfit.

However, in most Oriental *dojos* (schools)—and in too many of their American counterparts, so far as I am concerned—there is an almost worshipful respect shown for the teacher. Students aren't allowed to address the senior instructors directly. In fact, white belts—beginners—aren't allowed to speak to anyone but the grade above them, all the way up the line.

As far as I'm concerned, the white belt is one of the most important persons in a school. White belts come to the school, admit they're beginners, and put themselves into the hands of their instructors. That kind of trust merits respect in my view, a respect which should be mutual.

Today and Tomorrow

In the ten or fifteen years in which karate has been taught in the United States, the average student taking it has changed a great deal.

To be perfectly frank, many of the first karate students were street fighters, brawlers, and other rough types, the sort you'd expect to see hanging around a neighborhood boxing gym or loitering on street corners. That was the appeal of karate then. But very few of these people had the discipline to stick with the art and learn it thoroughly. The small number who did found themselves transformed into something very different from their original personalities.

These people learned both self-respect and respect for others. They stopped feeling they needed to test their courage on every possible occasion and began to live lives of nonconfrontation and nonviolence. In short, they became men—not examples of arrested adolescence.

Today the art attracts relatively few individuals with problems of this sort. Instead, the classes I see are filled with people who've already grown up—businessmen, professionals, skilled workers, students, housewives, artists—a sampling of society's best.

This makes sense. Karate is not for the simpleminded, the dense, the irresponsible, or undisciplined individual. It is a complex yet logical art. Because of that, I think, there are no stupid karateists. Furthermore, the more intelligent a person—the better his mind—the more quickly he will master the art and the more thoroughly he'll be able to learn it.

Not only has there been an increase in the quality

of karate students in the last decade or so, there's been an even more remarkable increase in the quality of teachers.

When I learned the art, beginning back in 1965, there weren't twenty-five black belts in my home state. The average grade of a karate teacher in New Jersey in those days was second- or third-degree black belt—and such people were about as competent as a good green belt (around the middle level) is today. I doubt that there were ten fifth-degree black belts on the East Coast in those days—and these people would barely have qualified as first-degree black belts according to current standards.

Today, qualified teachers abound. There are hundreds of black belts in almost every state of the Union—thousands in a few—and the level is going up every day.

Still, Americans have not gone far enough in making karate a truly American activity. The art has not been as much adapted to American needs and the American temperament as it should be, and as it can be.

Except in a relatively few enlightened schools, karate is taught as it was in the Orient decades—even centuries —ago. And its original customs are not simply honored in passing, they're worshipped. Americans have always respected foreign ideas, perhaps to a fault. I don't object to respectful admiration and even imitation of things foreign—as long as we really have something to learn. But when our prowess equals theirs, or begins to surpass it, then it's time to recognize the art is ours as much as it is theirs.

Americans have begun to do this—but only begun. For example, U.S. military men and policemen are now learning karate in large numbers, often taking from it what they feel is useful. Karate must adapt to American needs and abilities. After all, change and adaptation are at the very heart of karate's philosophy.

Along these lines, we might develop ways to train ourselves to use the weapons or tools we might have at hand, much as the ancient Okinawans learned to use the *bo*, the *tui-fa*, and the *sai*. Karate could be better adapted to the urban environment in which we live; karateists might be taught how to retain their balance on paved streets (rather than muddy fields) or how to make use of buildings and alleys. These adaptations would make karate more useful to us in the self-defense sense, and would also make it more of an American art.

Karate could be better for Americans than it already is. I want it to be perfect. The art is already extremely valuable in almost every aspect of life, and there's evidence that Americans are becoming more and more aware of this.

I don't know how many Americans are now taking or have taken some form of karate instruction. I don't think anyone does. But I've heard estimates ranging from between 3 million and 10 million people. And that number increases by hundreds of thousands every year. Karate is one of the fastest-growing physical activities in the United States and throughout the world.

The more black belts who graduate from commercial karate schools, the more new schools are set up. The art is now frequently taught for credit in college and universities and is becoming more and more popular in high schools, YMCAs, community gyms. I've heard it said that within ten years or so, one out of every three Americans will have some exposure to karate. Karate and the Western World are ready for each other today.

I see a time—and I believe it won't be long coming—when karate is as much a part of everyday American life as tennis, bicycling, jogging, or anything else you can name.

When that day comes, we'll be living in a different America. There will be less violence, I believe, since the concept of nonconfrontation will have made its way into the fabric of our society. There'll be less alienation, since people will feel more a part of the whole and relate better to each other. There'll be increased efficiency on the job and elsewhere, since people will more fully utilize their talents and abilities.

And we'll be a healthier nation, both mentally and physically.

Chapter 11
Choosing a Karate School

If you've decided that you want to try karate, there's one last step you'll have to take—picking a *dojo*, or karate school. The number of karate schools in America and in almost every country has quadrupled over the last four years. There's probably a school not far from your house. If you live in a metropolitan area, you might have several schools nearby.

Proximity to your home is important. If you have to drive an hour or more each way, you're not going to go regularly, no matter how gung-ho you may feel at the start. That first cold, snowy evening, you're going to snuggle up in your chair, turn on the TV or open a book, and think about how comfortable you are. Once you've missed a lesson, that long drive won't seem so fast and easy next time.

But don't just sign up at the closest *dojo*. There are several other points to consider. While the abundance of schools gives you increased opportunity to study karate, it also means that new, untried schools are opening daily. A good many schools have qualified teachers and are run professionally. But some are irresponsible, and disreputable.

Learning karate is an educational process. You should choose your school with the same care you'd choose a college. You should commit yourself to a course of study just as you'd enrol in a college program or correspondence school.

You should investigate the schools in your area thoroughly, because when you study karate, you're not only making a financial commitment to a school, you're entrusting yourself—or your child—to a teacher, a master. You want to be confident that he is worthy of that trust.

Your investigation should cover both the school and its master. Since the school is a reflection of the master, let's talk about his qualifications first.

There are two areas to consider when choosing a master: his credentials and his personal qualities.

Credentials

Credentials are rather difficult to judge. They are only as important as your ability to read and interpret them; and chances are, you can't. So don't be overly impressed if you walk into a *dojo* and see enough framed diplomas on the wall to furnish ten doctors' offices.

Meaningless certificates are easy to obtain. One of my students came in a few weeks ago and showed me a certificate he'd sent for by mail. He saw it advertised in a karate magazine, sent in a dollar, and received in return a black belt certificate signed in Chinese. That student could have framed that piece of paper and opened a school. Unless you are familiar with all the schools and masters in the country, and can read Chinese, how can you know what is important and what isn't? There's no harm in asking to see a master's certificate, but you certainly can't make a decision on that basis. You should also know that having a black belt doesn't necessarily qualify a person to teach karate. There is more to teaching than simply being a good karateist. Every master should have apprenticed with an established teacher before he begins teaching himself. He must be taught how to teach.

Personally, I feel a teacher should have at least five years' experience in the martial arts and two years as an assistant instructor before he becomes a full-fledged teacher. Obviously, these are not rigid rules. A committed, involved, talented person could be ready to teach with three years of experience. But these are good figures to use as a general guide when you're evaluating a master.

Just as having a black belt doesn't reveal anything about a master's teaching capabilities and experience, neither does it necessarily give you much information about his competence as a karateist. That's because there are several levels within the rank of black belt—from relatively low levels, where the student still has much to learn, to extremely advanced levels of mastery.

Even knowing which particular black belt degree a master holds doesn't give you definite information about his skills. There are many different systems of karate—more than forty are taught at present in the United

States and several hundred may yet come here from the Orient. A fifth *dan* black belt in one system doesn't mean the same as a fifth *dan* black belt in another. The level of skill required differs from system to system.

Let's assume you learn something about the various systems. Are you then prepared to evaluate the master's degree? Not really. Degrees are frequently bestowed upon masters for general contributions they may make to the martial arts. In addition, cross-grading, or giving honorary degrees, often occurs between different masters in various systems. There's really no way you can tell if a degree is honorary or whether it's a true reflection of the master's accomplishments in that particular system.

When you're choosing a master, the questions you might want to ask about his credentials will include: When did you start karate? With whom did you learn? Is your teacher still in business? where? When did you make black belt? Did you apprentice? with whom? for how long? How long have you been teaching?

You might also ask the master if he belongs to any martial arts organizations. I think he should be a member of at least one. To familiarize yourself with the names of organizations and schools, skim through a few of the trade magazines, *Black Belt* and *Kung Fu* in particular. These describe the associations and often indicate which are reputable and which aren't. If the master you're considering belongs to a particularly famous (or infamous) association, you might recognize the name. Some of the better-known and most respected associations at this writing are The Society of Black Belts of America, USKA, Jiu Jitsu, Black Belt Federation of America. Again, in this area, you'll probably have a tough time evaluating the answer, but there's no harm in asking.

The True Teacher

The personal qualities of a master will be much simpler for you to judge than his credentials, and they are really more important. A master can have all the training and experience in the world and still not be the kind of man you would want for your teacher.

You can evaluate the personal qualities of the master by talking to him, by watching him interact with his students, and by talking to his students about him. When you're talking to the master, don't let yourself be taken in by a charismatic personality or smooth rhetoric. The main thing you're looking for is his interest in you. He should be more concerned about helping you decide than he is about selling his school.

Is he open? Does he resent having to show his credentials and answer your questions? What are his other interests? If he is not a full-time instructor, what other job does he have? Does it also involve working with people? That last question might be a good sign.

Does he have patience? Does he want to end the conversation quickly, or is he willing to take the time to talk to you, to teach you right then and there, to give you enough information to help you make a good decision? If he is unwilling to spend time talking to you, he may be unwilling to give you the attention you require during a lesson. No one can learn karate—or anything else—from a teacher without patience. A patient teacher will also help the student develop the patience needed to perfect difficult techniques.

The master should be more than willing to let you observe his classes. Watch him with his students. There should be a very special rapport between them. Each should have respect for the other, since each is striving to improve himself through his art. The master and the student must rely on each other. The teacher can't be a teacher if he has no students and vice versa. A good master will treat his beginning students as respectfully as he treats his black belts. You don't want a school where beginners are looked down on.

The main purpose of the master should be to teach the student everything he is capable of learning. As you know, some masters, bound by the mystique and tradition of karate, never really divulge all. Some masters purposely hold back information, even if the student has advanced to the point where he should have it, so that the student will never know enough to challenge his teacher.

In my opinion, this is wrong. Just as it is a parent's duty fully to prepare his children for life, to encourage them to develop beyond the parent's own capabilities, if possible, so is it the master's duty to help his student develop fully in his art.

In addition to finding out how open and willing to teach the master is, you'll also want to look carefully to see that the students are not getting hurt or bruised in class. A good teacher will not hurt his students. He will be gentle. You should avoid a school that seems totally geared to violence, even if self-defense is your main reason for studying karate. Remember, the true karateist tries to avoid violence whenever possible.

When you watch the master with his class, ask yourself, Is this the kind of discipline I can learn? Is this a man I would trust? Could I put myself (or my child) in his hands with confidence? It's not a bad idea to watch a children's class in progress. How does the teacher relate to the children? He should encourage them, help to build their confidence, and treat them with respect. If you see a teacher talking down to a child, the chances are he's uncomfortable with children and isn't really the best instructor for them.

Pay attention to how formal the regime is. Does the master take an active interest in his students' progress, or is he removed, exalted, having little to do with the students? Does he have so many rules that the students aren't allowed to express themselves? Or is the class so informal that it is chaotic? Neither extreme is conducive to learning.

Be sure to speak with the students themselves after class. Ask them how they feel about the master. Are they afraid of him? If so, why? Are they in awe of him? Do they respect him? Do they like him? Do they feel he has helped them? What have they gotten from karate? Was that what they expected? How did they learn about the school? How long have they attended?

If a student says he heard about the school on a radio commercial and he's been attending for two weeks, ask someone else. If most students have come to the school by referral—on a friend's recommendation—you can bet you've found a good *dojo*. A referral student is a walking advertisement for a quality school.

A Thousand Systems

When you choose a master, you're also choosing his particular system. Deciding which system of karate is best for you is kind of like deciding which college to attend. There are hundreds of universities that will give you a bachelor of arts degree, but some of these colleges will fill your needs better than others.

I've already described the goals of karate and the benefits you can reasonably expect if you commit yourself to the art—no matter what system you learn. But different systems use different methods and stress various types of moves. Some emphasize kicking, while others rely mainly on jumping. Some systems depend on throwing and others stress punching.

Before you sign up for a course, you will probably want the master to describe his system. I hope he will also tell you if you are *not* going to be able to learn his system. Obviously, you're going to have a hard time in a jumping system if you're a real heavyweight. And if you're terribly underweight and have weak arms, you'll have difficulty throwing.

Some masters will modify their systems to accommodate different types of individuals. But others are very bound by tradition. They feel that the student must conform to the system.

You're going to want to learn the system that you're most comfortable with. Ideally, you should be able to choose it just as you'd choose a comfortable grip on your tennis racket. If there's more than one school in your area, you'll probably have an easier time finding a method that's suited to you. But if you have no choice, then the master's flexibility within his system could be very important.

Despite the common goals of all the martial arts systems, nearly all of them are in the war of competition. It might not be easy to find a master who is objective enough to tell you when his system is not the one that's best for you.

If you decide you like the master and the system, you still have one more judgment to make before signing up: how does the school itself shape up? You should consider the physical structure itself, the type of students who attend, the financial obligations the school requests, the time and travel required, and how long the school has been in business.

Physical Structure

The physical condition of the school is not of prime importance, but it can tell you something about the quality of the program and the type of people who run it, just as a house can tell you something about the people who live in it and how they run their lives.

If the building is kept up, you know that part of your money goes back into the school, that the owners really care about it. Many karate schools charge plenty but let the premises get shabby. This means that the owners are not investing in their business; they are pocketing all the profits without giving the students any benefits of their success.

This doesn't mean that a master shouldn't be making money. He should. He is a professional, and he should charge an appropriate fee for his services. He can't give lessons away because he must pay for his physical facilities. In addition, if the school is large and professional, it will have a teaching staff. The teachers must be adequately trained and paid if the high-quality standards of the school are to be maintained.

I'm not saying that the more expensive and lavish a karate school, the better it is. But you should avoid enrolling in a school that is suspiciously inexpensive, because you will probably not get the quality of instruction you need. Karate is something you will have all your life. Your money will not be wasted if you are taught well.

Be sure the school has the sanitary facilities that belong in any kind of gymnasium—locker rooms, showers, etc. In karate tradition, cleanliness, dignity, and an appropriate setting have always been an important part of the training.

Look at the practice area. During a class, is there enough room for everyone to work out, or are people constantly bumping into one another, even hitting one another because of lack of space? In karate, it is dangerous to get too close to one another, so enough space is important.

On the other hand, too much space isn't good either. If there's too much room, you won't have to pay attention to where the other students are or what they're doing. In karate, you have to relate your moves to the other person's moves.

If you don't see any mats on the floor, don't let that worry you. Mats are nice, but wooden floors are traditional in karate, and many fine schools do not use mats.

Your Fellow Students

When you observe, notice the size of the class. A reasonably large class is a good sign. Don't be taken in by the owner who says, "I keep my classes small so I can give each student a lot of personal attention." This is fine for a dancing class or a tennis class, but it's not fine for a karate class. A karate student needs a large variety of partners, for one thing. And a karate school that can't hold large classes probably doesn't have enough students to give that variety. Fifteen to fifty students in a single class is a good sign. The master will probably have an apprentice or two to assist him with a large group.

Return to observe the class the following week, or two weeks later, and see if the same people are there. A fast turnover indicates that the school can't hold on to its pupils. A relatively large, dedicated student body is an excellent sign of an effective school.

A large student body will have people of all ages, interests, professions, and educational levels. You'll probably feel comfortable there and find enough people who share your interests to make some friends. If a school doesn't have students you'd want to associate with, it isn't for you—even if it meets all the other requirements. If you're uncomfortable with your fellow students, or you don't like them, you won't be able to learn karate.

Mutual Obligations

You can't learn karate by showing up at the *dojo* whenever you are in the mood and paying at the door. To stay motivated after your initial determination wears off, or the work gets harder, you need to make a financial commitment. This not only benefits you, but it also benefits the school, by providing it with the income it needs to give first-rate instruction and maintain first-rate facilities.

Some obligation is a necessity. By signing up for a

modest number of lessons, you will be giving the school and karate a fair test. You can benefit from karate even if you study it only for a brief time, but I think three to six months is necessary for a fair trial.

A school should offer you some choice of programs. If a *dojo* offers only a five-year program, it's really taking advantage of the students. Even if a student has the motivation to stick with lessons for five years, he cannot know he's going to live in the area that long. Programs can be based on time limits, belt levels achieved, or number of lessons.

Let's say you enrol in a time program. Three months, unlimited lessons. That sounds good on the surface, but what if you get the flu and miss a week? Or what if you are sent to Philadelphia for two weeks? Suppose, for some reason or another, you can't make class more than once a week during those three months, and the owner has based his rate on the assumption you'll come three times a week? Some schools will give credit if you're out of town for part of the period you've signed up for, but others won't. Be careful before enrolling in this type of program. You deserve to get what you pay for.

I personally believe that a school should offer several programs based on a number of lessons, with no time limit. Of course, you should attend regularly, ideally twice a week, but you can space your lessons out however you want. It's best to begin with a smaller commitment.

Many schools will let you take a guest lesson. If they don't, they'll often give you a refund if you cancel after your first lesson. But a one-lesson trial is not really enough. You need some kind of full introductory course before you can get a true idea of what it means and how it feels to be a karateist.

Schools that base their programs on *guaranteed* achievement of certain belt levels regardless of real achievement are to be avoided. There are schools that have programs based on ridiculous promises: to become a black belt in two months, or become a master in fifteen lessons. Nobody can promise this. Everybody learns karate at a different rate. Some people may earn a first belt after twenty lessons; others may earn it after ten; some people may need fifty lessons.

Systems that promise you a certain belt after a certain amount of time or after a certain number of lessons won't make you a good karateist. Some people may deserve their belts on the promised schedule, but others may not. Teachers in these schools are too eager to give belts to those who don't earn them. You will want the satisfaction of knowing you truly deserve your belt. A belt that's been given away means nothing.

By the way, different belt colors mean different things in different systems. A white belt always signifies a novice, black belt always means a relative expert. But yellow, brown, or green can indicate any rank in between. If a school tells you you'll have a green belt in two months, you have no idea what rank that is, unless you ask.

If a school has been operating in one location for a number of years, say, five or more, it's likely to be a quality *dojo*. You have to be especially careful about a new school. Most of them are responsible, but every business has its con artists, and karate is no exception.

Some so-called masters open up a new school in a storefront, and three months later, after everybody in the area who ever wanted to learn karate has enrolled and paid for a lengthy program, they pack up and leave.

They go to another part of the country and pull the same stunt again. Five years later, they're back where they started. Nobody remembers them by that time. They use a different name and fleece the area again.

This is very hard on the karate student, and not only financially. Once you begin to learn one system, it isn't easy to enter another system at the same rank. When you do find another school, you've got to start from scratch.

Once a young college man came to enrol in my school. I asked him if he'd ever studied karate before, and he told me he'd had ten lessons at a school not far from mine. He'd paid for a twenty-week course, and after his first ten lessons, the school vanished. "I couldn't believe it," he said, "I showed up one night and the building was empty. Empty."

It didn't seem right that he should have to spend the money all over again. I gave him forty free lessons, and I'm glad I did. He's a black belt now, and he's referred a dozen students to the school during the time he's been studying with me.

Fortunately for all of us, teachers and students alike, this type of thing doesn't happen too often. But if the school you're considering is new, you'll want to be a little more careful about your evaluation of it. And you should be very reluctant to invest a large sum or to commit yourself to a long program.

In short, it's important to remember that when you're choosing a school, you're hiring a service. You have a right to competent, reliable instruction at a reasonable price. Your presence as a student is a compliment to the teacher and a reflection of your respect for him, his discipline, and his school.

Many local Ys or adult education programs now offer karate instruction. While these courses are sometimes taught by a professional who also has a school of his own, this doesn't happen often.

More than likely the teacher is a hobbyist, probably a black belt, but without any teacher training. Sometimes, though, the instructor will be an apprentice teacher from a local commercial *dojo*. This is better, but still not perfect, since the master will not be present to supervise the class. Quite frankly, I've seen too few YMCA or adult education courses that offer top-quality, fully trained instructors.

Usually the people who sign up for these courses are more interested in filling time than they are in learning karate. After eight weeks, they pick something else. They never really make a commitment to karate. Their interest in the art doesn't really grow after taking an adult ed course, because they haven't been taught by a real expert.

If you have a strong desire to learn karate, and there's no decent school (*dojo*) in your area, then by all means investigate the YMCA or adult ed program, evaluating it as much as possible by the criteria I've already discussed. Most often, I'd rather someone learn through these channels than not at all. In addition, smaller programs are improving all of the time.

But if you have a choice between a professional *dojo* or a Y, choose the karate school. Even if you want only a brief introduction to the art to find out how interested you are, you're better off there. You'll get a truer picture of what karate is really like, and you'll probably have a better teacher. You may pay a little more, but you'll be less likely to waste your money and your time.

I've tried in this book to give you some idea of what karate can do for both your mind and your body. I've tried to give you some idea of its history and its philosophy. Most of all, I've tried to show you why you should get involved in karate yourself. If you finish this book and go looking for a karate school, I'll feel my mission has succeeded.

As for you, you'll find yourself involved in something that can change your life for the better in more ways than you can count, something that will be with you as long as you live.

Bibliography

Adams, Andrew. *Ninja, the Invisible Assassins*. Los Angeles: O'Hara Publications, 1970.

Alain. *Yoga for Perfect Health*. New York: Pyramid Publications, 1961.

Applegate, Rex. *Kill or Get Killed*. Harrisburg, Pa.: Military Service Publishing Co., 1943.

Ardrey, Robert. *Territorial Imperative: A Personal Inquiry into the Animal Origins of Property and Nations*. New York: Atheneum, 1966; paperback, New York: Dell, 1968, 1971.

Arneil, Steve, and Dowler, Bryan. *Modern Karate*. Chicago: Henry Regnery, 1974.

Bancroft, Anne. *Religions of the East*. New York: St. Martin's Press, 1974.

Block, Alex Ben. *The Legend of Bruce Lee*. New York: Dell, 1974.

Bloomfield, Harold H.; Cain, Michael Porter; and Jaffe, Dennis T. *TM—Discovering Inner Energy and Overcoming Stress*. New York: Delacorte, 1975.

Burtt, E. A. *The Teachings of the Compassionate Buddha*. New York: New American Library, 1955.

Da Liu. *T'ai Chi Ch'uan and I Ching, A Choreography of Body and Mind*. New York: Harper & Row, 1972.

Devi, Indra. *Yoga for Americans*. Englewood Cliffs, N.J.: Prentice-Hall, 1959.

210

Draeger, Donn F., and Smith, Robert. *Asian Fighting Arts*. Tokyo and Palo Alto, Calif.: Kodansha International, 1969.

Feng, Gia-Fu, and Kirk, Jerome. *Tai Chi—A Way of Centering and I Ching*. New York: Collier, 1970.

Gluck, Jay. *Zen Combat*. New York: Bantam, 1962.

Griffith, Samuel B., trans. *Sun Tzu's Art of War*. London: Oxford University Press, 1963.

Haines, Bruce. *Karate's History and Traditions*. Rutland, Vt.: Charles E. Tuttle, 1968.

Howell, Maxwell L. *Chairman Mao's 4 Minute Physical Fitness Plan*. Millbrae, Calif.: Celestial Arts, 1973.

Huang, Chung-liang, Al. *Embrace Tiger, Return to Mountain*. Moab, Utah; Real People Press, 1973.

Janov, Arthur. *The Primal Scream*. New York: G. P. Putnam's, 1971.

Kim, Richard. *The Weaponless Warriors*. Los Angeles, Calif.: O'Hara Publications, 1974.

Kounovsky, Nicholas. *The Joy of Feeling Fit*. New York: E. P. Dutton, 1971.

Legge, James, as arranged by Clae Waltham. *I Ching, The Chinese Book of Changes*. New York: Ace, 1969.

Lorenz, Konrad. *On Aggression*. New York: Harcourt Brace Jovanovich, 1966.

Maisel, Edward. *Tai Chi for Health*. New York: Dell, 1963.

Minick, Michael. *The Kung Fu Exercise Book*. New York: Bantam, 1974.

Morehouse, Laurence E., and Gross, Leonard. *Total Fitness*. New York: Simon & Schuster, 1961.

Musashi, Miyamoto. *A Book of Five Rings*. Translated by Victor Harris. Woodstock, N.Y.: Overlook Press, 1974.

Nicol, C. W. *Moving Zen—Karate as a Way to Gentleness*. New York: William Morrow, 1975.

Oyama, Masutatsu. *Mastering Karate*. New York: Grosset & Dunlap, 1973.

Plee, H. D. *Karate by Pictures*. London: W. Foulsham, 1962.

Rawson, Philip, and Legeza, Laszlo. *Tao, the Eastern Philosophy of Time and Change*. New York: Avon, 1973.

Ross, Nancy Wilson. *The World of Zen*. New York: Vintage, 1960.

Selye, Hans. *Stress Without Distress*. Philadelphia and New York: J. B. Lippincott, 1974.

Smith, Robert W. *Secrets of Shaolin Temple Boxing.* Rutland, Vt.:
    Charles E. Tuttle, 1964.
Stryk, Lucien, and Ikemoto, Takashi. *Zen: Poems, Prayers, Sermons,
    Anecdotes, Interviews.* Garden City, N.Y.: Anchor, 1963.
Tegner, Bruce. *Bruce Tegner's Complete Book of Karate.* New
    York: Bantam, 1966.
Van Over, Raymond. *Taoist Tales.* New York: New American Li-
    brary, 1973.
Waley, Arthur, trans. and annotator. *The Analects of Confucius.*
    New York: Vintage, 1938.
Watts, Alan W. *The Way of Zen.* New York: Pantheon, 1957.
Wood, Ernest. *Yoga.* Middlesex, England: Penguin, 1959.

Index